Lori Ann Wood uses her ow
teaching us to how to hold gr
vine Detour, Lori Ann Wood artfully weaves whimsical childhood stories with dramatic cardiac journal entries and Christian theology to offer the reader lasting lessons in faith. Read this book either as a forty-day journey or as one sitting binge—either way, you will return to it again and again for her wit and wisdom. There are little lessons everywhere and hope for everyone.

—Kathy Izard, author of
The Hundred Story Home and *The Last Ordinary Hour*

I've worked with many promising writers over the years who have gone on to accomplish great feats, but few have been as talented, hardworking, and endearing as Lori Ann Wood. She writes with the kind of authenticity that simply cannot be taught, and her work is punctuated by haunting turns of phrases with the power to rattle teeth. I cannot wait to get my hands on *Divine Detour* and recommend it to the many, many people I know in need of its message.

—Jonathan Merritt, contributing writer for *The Atlantic*
and author of *Learning to Speak God from Scratch*

Lori Ann Wood courageously shares her journey with vulnerability and grace. She walks boldly into the unknown and in the process teaches us to do the same. This is a gift to anyone struggling with uncertainty, health issues, or trying to find footing in the world.

—Margaret Feinberg, author of *More Power to You*

Through a series of forty deeply personal essays, Lori Ann Wood shows us that questions and struggles do not have to weaken our faith, but can instead strengthen it. This book offers strong encouragement for those going through difficult life and faith challenges.

—Brian Allain, founder of *Writing For Your Life, Publishing in Color,*
How to Heal Our Divides, and *Compassionate Christianity*

When we're asking hard questions, we just want answers. But what we really need is to know we're not alone, God is good no matter what happens, and our story isn't finished yet. Lori Ann Wood is a wise friend and fellow traveler who will walk with you toward those truths and whose words will give you newfound hope no matter where you are on your journey right now.

—Holley Gerth, *Wall Street Journal* Bestselling Author of *What Your Mind Needs for Anxious Moments*

My journey with Lori began in her young adult years with routine medical care and the birth of her children. She was a steady, loving, and reliable mother who rarely seemed rattled or frustrated. My true understanding of Lori, however, was born later when she developed a chronic, debilitating condition that required mental and spiritual strength and confidence. This book reveals her gift as a writer, her calm confidence in her faith, and her quiet acceptance of her own human limitations. It also provides the structure that has allowed her faith to grow with her life struggles. She has managed to weave her challenges and her belief into literature, providing solace and comfort from God. Reading her book is a recharge for pure, calm faith.

—Gary A. Neaville, M.D., Family Practice/OB

Tucked within these pages are an exploration of three very important questions we all ask when our lives are interrupted by an unwanted event, or when things are going the opposite of what we hoped. I loved the depth of encouragement, hope, and words found within Lori's book, *Divine Detour*.

—Suzanne (Suzie) Eller, bestselling author of twelve books, co-host of *More Than Small Talk* podcast, and host of *Prayer Starters* podcast

Wilderness is not only a kind of topography, it is a kind of experience, one characterized by hardship, disorientation, and unknowing. In *Divine Detour*, Lori Ann Wood guides us through the wilderness landscapes of faith as a seasoned traveler. Similar to Joseph's life taking an unwanted and unexpected detour to Egypt removing all support systems of family, familiar territory and daily routine, Lori Ann transparently recounts her feelings of abandonment, disappointment, grief, vulnerability, and fear as she journeys with a life-threatening disease that brought the primary questions of existence and meaning to her heart's inmost chamber.

In forty essays using engaging stories, theological reflection, and journal entries that capture significant moments in her encounter with impermanence, Lori Ann skillfully and pastorally accompanies us into our own wilderness experience as we ask the recurring questions of uncertainty and fear that accompany our humanity. *Divine Detour* is a supportive companion for all whose hearts have the courage to ask aloud the ultimate life questions we all carry silently, fearfully, and unnecessarily alone.

—Ross Cochran, Ph.D., Professor of Practical Theology and author of *Not Off Limits: Questions You Wish You Could Ask at Church*

In *Divine Detour,* Lori Ann Wood articulates the honest emotions of someone on a health journey, unsought and unwanted. Faced with being swept under by a life-threatening heart condition or using it to grow spiritually, Lori chose the latter. The result is this book, written for fellow sojourners whose lives have been disrupted by God. I was one of them, given a cancer diagnosis ten years ago, so I know trite treatment and pat answers when I see them. This book has none of that. There's meat on these bones. Readers will connect with Lori's stories, grow by her insights, and be encouraged to trust God in their own detours.

—Sherri Langton, Associate Editor, *Bible Advocate Magazine*

When I first met Lori Ann, I was impressed with her grace, her gentleness, and her ageless beauty. I had no idea she carried a secret in her chest that had, fairly recently at that point, changed her life forever. As I got to know her, I became even more in awe of her. How does she carry it so well? So effortlessly? But the truth about Lori Ann is that this enduring strength comes not from herself, but from her Savior. *Divine Detour* is not an account of how amazing she is (though that's true too) but, rather, how amazing God is. Lori Ann orients herself by the Truth of the Word and the love of Christ. There is no self-pity here. Only humility, joy, and palpable peace. Though I am not walking the same life road as Lori Ann, I long to follow her as she follows Jesus. Her heart, and this lovely book, are graceful, gentle, and agelessly beautiful.

—Hannah C. Hall, author of
Thirsty: 12 Weeks of Drinking Deeply from God's Word

Divine Detour is more than a book about a devastating diagnosis and the day-to-day battle that ensues. It's also more than a book about faith. *Divine Detour* is a testimony of the goodness of God—a God who invites us to ask the hard questions in the hard places, so we can find Him in the answers. Lori Ann Wood shares the wisdom she's discovered with a gentle, authentic voice that draws you close and makes you feel less alone. Her soft words will soothe and strengthen your weary soul as you journey your own detour in life. Come discover the harmony of gratitude and grief, the beauty of *hesed* love (one of my favorite words), and the incompatibility of regret and grace. Reading this book will be a forty-day journey, perhaps a detour from your other reading, you'll be glad you took.

—Andy Lee, author of *Radiant Influence: How an Ordinary Girl Changed the World* and *A Mary Like Me: Flawed Yet Called*

As a part of her medical team, I knew Lori was brave and had a deep faith. But this book blew me away. God's triumphant goodness and unwavering faithfulness are on full display as she walks us through her difficult diagnosis and the uncertainty of life. I recommend this to all who, like me, struggle with doubt, worry, and control.

—Heather Rothrock Heltemes, APRN-CNP, Cardiology

Lori Ann Wood is a very special writer—she has a unique and beautiful way of exploring the hard questions that most believers wrestle with while compassionately inviting them to journey along with her to discover the Truth of God's character. Walking through her own devastating experience has given her a concrete faith—solidified in the fire of life's most difficult circumstances—making her incredibly relatable to any reader. If you hope to grow in your faith, find God amid your darkest trials, and fall more deeply in love with your Savior—*Divine Detour* should be on your reading list.

—Sandi Warner, Editor in Chief of *The Joyful Life Magazine*

Lori Ann has a wondrous way of enveloping you in engaging personal story, befriending you in collective hardship, and generously inviting you to share in the bounty of her hard-won discoveries. This collection of approachable, Scripture-rich essays helped gently shift the perspective of my own divine detours—beholding them more appropriately for what they are (and are not).

We are a people thirsty for answers, yet Lori Ann highlights the beautiful juxtaposition in celebrating the courage to question. For, in the rugged desert terrain of difficulty, where solutions are hardest to decipher, it is a desperate inquisitive posture that best fortifies wobbly faith. The intimate health desert she has traversed in order to unearth these insights for our mutual edification is nothing short of remarkable.

—Tiffany Edmonds, Managing Editor of *The Joyful Life Magazine*

Lori Ann Wood has poured her heart into these pages, sharing her tragic journey with transparent honesty. If you're struggling with any kind of disappointment or disillusionment in your life, then *Divine Detour* will be a welcome guide for your soul! Lori Ann is an engaging, relatable storyteller drawing deep from Scripture and her own suffering. She wrestles with the painful questions we all ask and helps us come out the other side with a stronger hope and faith—and deeper relationship with God. A great companion for anyone who is questioning their faith and the goodness of God. Every page will bring you hope and lead you to the God who has your life in His hands.

—Shelly Esser, Editor of *Just Between Us Magazine*

No one enjoys hearing the word *failure* connected to our physical or spiritual health. Yet over six million Americans experience failure of the heart—the major pumping organ needed to sustain life. Regardless of contributing factors, people living with Heart Failure (HF) struggle with guilt, loss of life as it once was, and the teeter-totter of heart function improvement (hope) versus decline (hopelessness) with every diagnostic test and physician encounter.

Many Christians question God's love, grace, and mercy. Lori Ann Wood understands. She questioned God, too.

This collection of essays provides readers with a transparent and brutally honest self-reflection from an educated Christian woman secure in faith, career, and purpose. Taking a detour on unfamiliar roads triggers angst, fear, and loss of control. How can a Christian doubt God's love and purpose? Questions fly and Lori is courageous enough to give voice to the unspeakable, lay heartache before the Lord, seek His response, and unselfishly share answers to comfort others.

When one recognizes a detour in life to be divine, change happens. God's purpose, grace, and love for Lori is manifested by the gift of heart failure. God took a physical condition and created a sensitive, loving author willing to change course to touch the lives of many.

Ephesians 2:10 (NKJV) "For we are His workmanship, created in Christ Jesus for good works, which God prepared beforehand so that we should walk in them."

—Donna D. Kincheloe, DNP, RN, CHFN, CMSRN, Certified Heart Failure Nurse and author of *I Never Walk the Halls Alone*

Lori Ann was the sickest patient a veteran cardiologist had ever seen. Her chances of survival were slim, yet she did survive. She is that rare soul who took the worst life can give and persevered through it, but she did even more than that. She wrote *Divine Detour: The Path You'd Never Choose Can Lead to the Faith You've Always Wanted*, generously showing you and me how we, too, can get through the hard trials of life. These forty readings will help you renew your faith and give you the courage you need to move forward no matter what.

—Chad R. Allen, longtime publishing professional and founder of *BookCamp*

Taking us through her most poignant moments in *Divine Detour*, Lori Ann Wood shares the sometimes sweet and other times devastating life events that she has skillfully woven into an intimate dialogue between herself and God about purpose, meaning, and faith. As a WomenHeart Champion, Lori's desire to share her journey with us is yet another expression of her commitment to using her life experience to walk with others in their own journeys from heartbreak and diagnosis to acceptance and action. Lori's *Divine Detour* is an invitation not just to women with heart disease but to every person to lean into their faith, poke and prod it and question it when faced with the unexpected and unwanted detours in life. You will enjoy Lori's forty beautiful essays that merge to a glorious mosaic of inspiration, acceptance, and love.

—Celina E. Gorre, Chief Executive Officer of WomenHeart

DIVINE DETOUR

The path you'd never choose can lead to the faith you've always wanted

With You on the Journey,
Lori Ann Wood

LORI ANN WOOD

ST JOSEPH, MISSOURI USA

DIVINE DETOUR

Paperback ISBN: 978-1-936501-75-5
Hardcover ISBN: 978-1-936501-76-2

 Published by CrossRiver Media Group, 4810 Gene Field Rd. #2, St. Joseph, MO 64506. Crossrivermedia.com

For more on Lori Ann Wood, please visit her website, LoriAnnWood.com.

Editor: Debra L. Butterfield
Cover Designer: Tamara Clymer
Cover Photography: Photo 217824013 © Konstanttin | Dreamstime.com

Printed in the United States of America.

For the family that made me:

For my parents who introduced me to
faith, grace, and resilience;
For my siblings who share my stories;
For my children and grandchild,
who give my writing urgency and purpose;

Above all, for my husband who, even when we were living the story
we didn't want, always believed God really was up to something.

Contents

Foreword

Lori Wood came to my clinic seven years ago for the first time with her husband pushing her in a wheelchair. I had a sinking feeling when I met her that she would not survive, despite all my years of training as a heart failure and transplant cardiologist.

She was frail, losing muscle mass, and had a big, baggy heart with a strength of just 6 percent. Most heart failure medications decrease blood pressure. Lori's blood pressure was already extremely low, even on the minimal doses she was taking, making me wonder how I could increase them enough to make any difference at all. I had a few options that rushed through my head: I could take her to surgery for a mechanical heart, place her on the heart transplant waiting list, or I could stick with medications. After examining her, I knew the output from her heart was somehow adequate since her hands were still warm. I also knew that although I could use advanced heart failure care options, there was a slight chance her heart could strengthen and her prognosis might be even better if I relied solely on medical therapy. Was this realistic given the enormous size of her heart? I had an impossible choice to make. Unsure if recovery was even realistic, I asked if they could return to Ohio since she lived in Arkansas and my medical practice was at the Cleveland Clinic. The answer was yes, and we began our long journey together.

Throughout the years I have treated Lori, I have been drawn in by her determination to face every dark, unknown path in front of her. She has always forged ahead, wherever it led. Medical prognosis was no match for her will to face the daunting problems head-on. She seemed empowered and even strengthened by embracing the questions.

This is the story of a brave woman, a loving husband, and the amazing cooperation and trust between her local medical team and myself. But it is also the story of undeniable direction. I am still not sure how we all met. (Some might suspect it was the luck of the draw or perhaps they somehow knew my research focus was heart failure in women.) At so many steps, the story could have taken a very different turn. Lori's diagnosis was established after multiple visits to healthcare facilities for shortness of breath and failed treatment for infection with antibiotics. By the time she went to an emergency room she was in severe heart failure with respiratory distress and kidney failure. Once admitted to her local hospital, she was given life-saving inotrope support. This treatment caused a 35-beat run of ventricular tachycardia that could easily have been deadly. She was discharged with a life vest capable of shocking her heart from outside her body. A few days later, Lori and her husband traveled to my office that first time by plane. The flight was delayed and almost cancelled because she passed out after boarding. Paramedics treated her on the tarmac and advised her not to fly. The risky decision was made by her team of doctors to continue to Cleveland Clinic because her options and chances were limited otherwise.

Every three months Lori made her way to Cleveland and between visits had amazing care by her local cardiologist Dr. Christopher Simpson who gradually increased medications based on my recommendations. In retrospect, Dr. Simpson was incredibly brave because Lori's blood pressure remained low. With time and therapy, her heart function rose from 6 percent to 16 percent but did not further improve until she had a biventricular pacemaker implanted in 2016 for a left bundle branch block. Her heart strengthened and its size shrunk significantly.

The visits to Cleveland became fewer and our focus changed. Lori wanted to be an advocate for other women with heart disease. She requested I write a recommendation letter for her to become a member of WomenHeart, a national patient advocacy group that provides emotional support, education, and representation on Capitol Hill.

How odd, we both had joined the same group for the same purpose a few years apart. I joined the scientific advisory committee for WomenHeart when they were preparing a Congressional report, *The Top Ten Cardiovascular Questions for Women with Heart Disease.* Lori independently recognized the value of WomenHeart and is now a trained Champion who assists other women with heart disease.

We have made podcasts together and developed a strong relationship which has become a great friendship. I have had a front row seat to see Lori face a difficult diagnosis and dark days up close. Through it all, I knew she was a person of faith. It is my honor to introduce to you this amazing woman. For seven years I have wanted to know what else, besides world-class medical intervention, has kept her going. Now I know, and true to her spirit, she wants to help you along your unknown path, too.

The book you're holding is a testament to the will and faith of my patient and friend. It is the culmination of several years of treatment and questions. It is Lori's gift from her heart to yours.

Eileen Hsich, MD
Medical Director Heart Transplant
Cleveland Clinic

Introduction

Every life experiences a moment when the story breaks into two pieces: pre-tragedy and post-tragedy. When there suddenly becomes a *before* and an *after*. When the carefully planned journey takes a decided detour. This was mine.

• • • • •

"If we're lucky, it's pneumonia."

Our beloved family physician's words hung like thick fog in the bright exam room. Taking the stethoscope out of his ears, he led us down the long hallway to the X-ray lab.

After a week with what I thought was the flu, I had finally made an appointment with my family doctor. My husband was with me. It was Black Friday and rather than go shopping with our daughters, he opted to drive me. We had expected it to be quick and rather routine, perhaps a steroid shot at worst. We had made a bet about how soon we'd be back home that day: *Would I miss the door busters altogether?*

It would be more than two weeks before I made it home, and I would be a different person when I finally did walk through that door. I was wounded, yet on the verge of an understanding of faith that I may never have experienced outside the tragedy that was unfolding. I crossed that familiar threshold disillusioned and frightened, begging for answers to the big life questions of worry, doubt, and control.

My primary care doctor would later describe that day in his office as the worst day of his professional career. He couldn't believe he'd missed it all those years. Honestly, the subtle symptoms didn't alarm me, and I never reported the shortness of breath, fatigue, or inability to exercise. I attributed the symptoms to "getting older," and "being out of shape" compared to my marathon-running husband. So, my physician never knew about the warning signs.

This doctor was more like an old friend or family member I saw only a few times a year. He had burned pre-cancerous moles from my back, prescribed antibiotics for strep, and delivered my babies. He knew and remembered the health histories of both of my parents, though he'd never met them. He simply loved taking care of people.

That's why it hit him so hard when the chest X-ray showed something else. Something much worse. I was diagnosed with severe idiopathic dilated cardiomyopathy, a form of heart failure brought on by an unknown cause.

For lack of a more glaring suspect, doctors assume a virus had attacked my heart. My heart was functioning at just 6 percent the day I walked into my doctor's office. I spent fourteen days in the hospital, most of it in ICU, as doctors worked around the clock to save my life. All of this despite having no risk factors, no family history, low blood pressure, low cholesterol levels, and a recent life insurance evaluation declaring I had less than 3 percent chance of ever developing heart disease.

I was flown to the Cleveland Clinic where I became my cardiologist's most critical patient for a year and a half. Later I learned that I was the sickest patient she had treated in her sixteen years as Director of the Women's Heart Failure Clinic and as Associate Director for the Heart Transplant Program at the Cleveland Clinic, the top heart hospital in the nation. Not the badge I was hoping to earn. Eventually, I was implanted with a Biventricular CRT-D, a combination pacemaker/internal defibrillator.

Thousands of people prayed for me around the clock despite a grim prognosis and sympathetic tears from every doctor we encountered. Contrary to what the rational part of my brain wanted to do, I held on tight and trusted. Miraculously, I survived. Against all medical odds, my heart function was temporarily restored sixteen months later.

But as heart failure goes, my condition has experienced ups and downs since then.

And as the Christian walk goes, so has my faith.

My story is not fully written. Since that remarkable reversal, my heart function has dropped twice and is now stable at a lower plateau. I am learning more every year about the unpredictability of this condition. Heart failure is a chronic, progressive disease. There is no cure. For most, medical science can manage the symptoms. For some, they can slow the progression. Doctors believe I will likely need a heart transplant in the future.

I still struggle with questions, almost daily. But rather than seeing them as a threat to my faith, I see them as a lifeline to keeping it.

The post-diagnosis years have taken me on a faith detour I never saw coming. As a longtime believer, I felt profoundly disappointed. I wanted answers, but more importantly, I needed permission to ask the questions.

This forty-day book is a result of my pursuit to embrace the questions and navigate the desert I've found myself in.

In Scripture, the number forty represents trial or testing. Moses fasted forty days in the wilderness, the Israelites wandered forty years in the desert, Noah survived forty days and nights in the flood, Elijah suffered forty days without food or water at Mount Horeb, the spies spent forty days scouting out the land of Canaan, Jonah warned that in forty days Nineveh was approaching doom.

Perhaps the most well-known forty-day period is the one Jesus endured in the desert before beginning his public ministry, described in Matthew 4:1–11:

> Then Jesus was led by the Spirit into the wilderness to be tempted by the devil. After fasting forty days and forty nights, he was hungry. The tempter came to him and said, "If you are the Son of God, tell these stones to become bread."

> Jesus answered, "It is written: 'Man shall not live on bread alone, but on every word that comes from the mouth of God.'"
>
> Then the devil took him to the holy city and had him stand on the highest point of the temple. "If you are the Son of God," he said, "throw yourself down. For it is written: '"He will command his angels concerning you, and they will lift you up in their hands, so that you will not strike your foot against a stone."'
>
> Jesus answered him, "It is also written: 'Do not put the Lord your God to the test.'"
>
> Again, the devil took him to a very high mountain and showed him all the kingdoms of the world and their splendor. "All this I will give you," he said, "if you will bow down and worship me."
>
> Jesus said to him, "Away from me, Satan! For it is written: 'Worship the Lord your God, and serve him only.'"
>
> Then the devil left him, and angels came and attended him. (NIV)

Satan's whispers during that foray into the desert were meant for more than just a good Bible story. Those whispers continue to echo through the deserts every believer will face in this life. And they manifest in deep faith questions.

My story involves a testing period as well. I have spent some time in that desert. But I have also had my hand directly in the hand of Jesus during these days, as One who knows the territory personally. In fact, as I live and learn through my chronic illness, my journey has been surprisingly parallel to the questions Jesus wrestled with during his forty days in the desert. I suspect yours has as well, regardless of which detour you have trekked.

When the Enemy tempted Jesus to turn the stones into bread to satisfy his physical hunger, he was whispering something to Jesus that he often whispers to us in our physical suffering: *Survival is most important. Do whatever it takes to make sure you are comfortable in this life. Nothing else is guaranteed but what you can see and feel and taste here.*

Our immediate concerns matter most. As believers, we are left with a Question of Worry. Question #1: Is this life all there is?

Then Satan tried the second whisper, bending down to Jesus's ear and to ours: *Jump and see if God will suspend natural laws to save you. God will catch you if He loves you. He won't let you get hurt. A good God won't let His child suffer. If He does, He must not care.* We struggle with the Question of Doubt. Question #2: Is God always good?

Finally, Satan asked Jesus to worship him instead of God in exchange for wealth in this life. The Enemy has whispered that lie to many of us. *Your life plan is at least as good as God's, probably better. Besides, you don't have to be all-in with God. You can still run your part of the show.* We come face to face with a Question of Control, especially when we end up in the desert. Question #3: Is God's plan enough?

These whispers of the Enemy can hound us in our tedium, or they can haunt us in our trials. Either way, these three questions must eventually be addressed. Just as the Spirit led Jesus into that dark desert to be tested, it is part of the plan for us to be tested as well. It is a faith-building gift God allows in every Christian: the opportunity to question, to engage our belief, and to choose Him again and again.

This book contains forty essays to spur your own encounter with these three life questions.

Though my journey through the desert is not yet complete, the detour is now the expected route. My everyday faith is tempered by knowing that He doesn't always behave like I want Him to. However, God's abundant grace encourages my questions along the way. And more importantly, His Spirit never stops pursuing my inquisitive heart.

Forty is trial, but God never leaves us in our trials. Forty also indicates deep transformation is coming. Forty signifies God's environment for change. Forty represents a new set of instructions for a new phase in life. Forty is testing, but it is also fulfillment, of plans and promises, long-suffered and hard-fought, that have come to reality. The most celebrated end to a forty-day period happened forty days after the resurrection. The restored Jesus ascended as hundreds, maybe thousands, of new believers celebrated His earthly existence, a job well done, and an eternal homecoming. The same Jesus who faced the forty days in the desert encountered Glory on the other side of another forty-day period.

This is our God. The God who comes full circle from testing to triumph, never leaving us with a story unfinished. While these forty essays represent forty days, they don't have to be forty consecutive days. Take whatever forty "days" you want, over whatever period feels right. Each of us will wrestle with these questions at a different pace. I pray these forty days, however you choose to encounter them, will help you confront the three life questions and move you toward your own triumph, on a journey deeper into the heart of our amazing God.

• • • • •

A NOTE ABOUT FORMAT

The book you are holding is not a chronological memoir of my heart failure journey.

Instead, you will find forty stand-alone story-driven essays, organized among the three life questions. Jesus used stories to deliver His most important lessons. Jesus knew we figure out life in short bursts, in single scenes, in sound bites, rather than in novel form. He knew that's how we encounter faith as well.

As you read through these essays, you will find different parts of my story (and related journal entries) sprinkled among the three questions. These story fragments will not necessarily appear in the order they occurred. This is by design.

While life is lived on a linear timeline, faith is not developed in the same way. It's not how I've grasped hold of belief, and I'm guessing it's not the way you have, either. In this book you will find the Question of Worry may include events relating to my early diagnosis, my eventual device, my sudden improvement, my subsequent downturn, and my lower plateau. The same with the other questions, Doubt and Control—I confronted each question in all parts of my journey. I never want to give the impression that a question is resolved and tabled, and that we move on to other "higher level" questions. Instead, as believers we face the same three questions throughout life. We tackle Worry only to question it again and again.

To be honest, it seemed at first logical and tidy to detail the events in order and label the sections with the alliteration, *Diagnosis*, *Device*, and *Downturn*. Then I realized this book has always been more about developing your faith than about detailing my medical events. I hope this format speaks to you and gives you permission to continue questioning, in all three areas, wherever you are along your own divine detour.

Take hold of your uncertainties. Let's step out together in inquisitive faith. I'm with you on this journey.

A Question of Worry

Days 1–13

• • • • •

Jesus's Desert Dilemma

"The tempter came to him and said, 'If you are the Son of God, tell these stones to become bread'" (Matthew 4:3 NIV).

What We Hear

My top priority is my immediate physical need.

Life Question

Is this life all there is?

DAY 1

A Season of Grief and Gratitude

"You just sunk our friendship!"

My older sibling laid the harsh words on me early one Christmas break. I was a little unclear about what I had done, but I knew it was bad, and this faux pas had created a big loss. We could no longer be friends. Ever again.

Crushed, I did the only thing my five-year-old self knew to do, the only thing that was in my control at the time.

I ran away from home.

I packed my Holly Hobbie suitcase with a handful of saltines, two pieces of leftover Halloween candy, and three carrots to balance it out. Then, grabbing my coat, I headed to the most desolate and private place in my known universe: the pasture next to the house.

As I walked deeper into the dry landscape, I noticed a structure in the distance and hatched an idea. I climbed the cold metal steps to the top of an oil storage tank that sat in the middle of the pasture. Pretending it was my own house, I unpacked my suitcase and set up my kitchen. I felt self-sufficient.

Aside from a few Angus steers, I was totally alone. Or so I thought. As I turned to glance back nostalgically at my not-so-distant childhood home, a truck barreled toward me in a whirlwind of dust.

I imagined it was Dad, coming to rescue me or beg me to reconsider.

It wasn't.

Instead, an oil field worker arrived, unwelcome, at my new residence. He scolded me, warned me of certain injury or possible death, and threatened to tell my parents. In deep fear and a tinge of humiliation, I packed up and headed home.

Even in the glow of the freshly decorated Christmas tree, I felt the scowl of the offended sibling across the table that evening. Grateful to be back with my family, out of danger (and out of trouble), I was still feeling the grief that took me there in the first place. I struggled with that mix of feelings the entire holiday. It was a difficult place to be.

GRIEF MIXED WITH GRATITUDE

Following that runaway incident, I lived in the tension between grief and gratitude. Many live in this tight space, holding both in equal measure. Sometimes the whole world has felt too heavy. At least mine has:

Grief for the loss of both parents within four months.

Grief for the loss of a quarantined year that seemed to evaporate from my certainly shortened life.

Grief for graduations, gatherings, hugs, that should have been.

But alongside my grief sits a corresponding helping of gratefulness:

Gratitude for extended family and understanding friends, for feeling alive at the far end of a harsh prognosis.

Gratitude for the existential push to start pursuing a delayed dream.

Gratitude for God-given medical expertise.

I am perplexed to feel both emotions so strongly; it seems almost hypocritical. But I am also struck that the things I am most grateful for reflect what I am grieving deepest. Just like that attempted move to the pasture.

Francis Weller says it is possible and even beneficial to experience both grief and gratitude, "The work of the mature person is to carry grief in one hand and gratitude in the other and to be stretched large by them."

Grief and gratitude are not an either/or proposition. We can be grateful and still be grieving. One was never meant to negate or supersede the other.

GRATITUDE NEEDS GRIEF

Grief and gratitude can coexist, and maybe they have to. Maybe we can never appreciate fullness without loss. Maybe they are actually partners in bringing the realization of God's mercy into our hearts.

"Grief and gratitude are kindred souls, each pointing to the beauty of what is transient and given to us by grace." —Patricia Campbell Carlson

It's the human condition. Songs have been sung about it, poems have been penned about it, and hearts have been hurt by it. You don't know what you've got until it's gone. Health, family, grand plans. As I get older, I am increasingly grateful for all those things that go missing because their absence reminds me of how blessed I am to have had them at all.

"It is the gift of grief, the price we have to pay for relationships and the deep love for those we have lost, that makes it possible to be grateful." —Adam Rabinovitch

My journal entry while I was first in ICU:

After the dust settled on the immediate life-saving measures, I learned that, by medical opinion, I likely will not live five years. Statistics say 50 percent of people with any type of heart failure die within five years. For those with a BNP at the drastic level of mine, only 50 percent survive ninety days after being released from their initial hospital stay. Ninety percent of those die within a year. It's as if I'm standing outside the window of my own life, and it's not a pretty scene. My numbers are so bad and my chances look even worse.

The future is still not any clearer than it was that day in ICU. It's not how I hoped it would be, but I'm thankful for what it is. And acknowledging that never discounts the grief for the way I wish things could be.

One year represents 20 percent of the life expectancy I'd been given. Woven into one twelve-month segment were the perfect opportunities to talk deeply with my dad as I sat at his hospice bed, and with my mother, my siblings, and my children, as we planned then processed funerals. Without the losses that were part of that year, none of that would have happened.

FEELING SEEN IN OUR GRIEF

So much of our lives can be summarized by a statement Jesus made. "You do not realize now what I am doing, but later you will understand" (John 13:7 NIV).

Jesus's own mother must have felt this too.

Young, unwed Mary expecting the Savior of the world was surely grieving the loss of her planned life and guarded reputation. "How can this be?" (Luke 1:34 NKJV).

For all of us managing our expectations, grief comes in the confusing, challenging, "not realizing" phase. And it can be a lonely place to be.

If we feel alone and unseen, grief can become polluted with self-focused guilt and regret. (I secretly wanted *someone* to notice I was missing from the house that half-hour I was in the pasture. Otherwise, what would be the point?)

But if we feel seen, grief can be felt and processed in light of a bigger picture. And gratitude can emerge from that dark place. Even when we're living the story we didn't want.

Mary felt seen by her cousin Elizabeth and wrote a song of praise and thanksgiving, "The Magnificat," just weeks after the shock of the angel's baby announcement. "My soul glorifies the Lord, and my spirit rejoices in God my Savior, for he has been mindful of the humble state of his servant" (Luke 1:46–48a NIV).

These post-diagnosis years, difficult as they've been, I have felt seen. By my family, my friends, professionals in the medical field. But most importantly, by *El Roi*, the God Who Sees. And it has made all the difference in how my grief has held space for soul-soothing gratitude.

Author Kelly Buckley writes about grieving with gratitude. "Gratitude does not change the pain of the loss. But it does alleviate some of the suffering." Indeed, with the help of community, it has.

Running away to the pasture, it was easy to get back. But so much of that was pretend, and most of what we're now living is not. Still, that grief we are carrying into a new season, or trying to escape as we head into a new year, can be the truest springboard to gratitude.

And it all starts by being seen in our grief. Maybe first by a fellow sufferer online or a quarrelsome family member, or even a stranger in an oil truck.

But ultimately, by our good and gratitude-worthy God.

DAY 2

Soft Endings

The summer after second grade, I wanted two things more than I wanted to breathe: to finally attend overnight 4-H camp like my older siblings, and to own a miniature dachshund. In the ’70s, they both cost about $35, which was a chunk of change. I knew it, and my dad knew it, so he said I could have my choice.

Of course, I chose the dog.

She was perfect. Tiny, tan, smooth, and wiggly. Missy and I had the best summer together. But inevitably, summer ends and third grade calls. About a week into the new school year, I was running late. I usually played with Missy for about fifteen minutes each morning before I left. I still didn’t have my routine down of feeding Missy, feeding myself, and catching the 7:10 a.m. bus. Feeling rushed, I knocked Missy down with my shoe when she wanted to play. I grabbed my jacket and headed out the door, ignoring her sweet, pleading eyes.

That afternoon a message came from the office into my third-grade world via the intercom box above the classroom flag. The secretary’s garbled voice relayed to my teacher that my dad was there to pick me up. I knew that was not a good sign. We lived seventeen miles from town, and Dad didn’t casually drop by my school in the middle of the day. Immediately, my mind went to the worst thing I could imagine. I walked toward the office. *God, please don’t let this be about Missy.* I crawled into Dad’s pickup and squeezed the worn vinyl seat. *God, please don’t let this be about Missy.*

But it was. She had been hit by a car while I was at school.

UNEXPECTED LASTS

My nine-year-old soul was crushed.

I regretted that our final encounter wasn't a happy one. Mostly, I remember being sad that I didn't know it was the last time I would see her.

That was my first taste of the reality James described as a fog that appears for a brief time and then evaporates. "Why, you do not even know what will happen tomorrow. What is your life? You are a mist that appears for a little while and then vanishes" (James 4:14, NIV).

Moments evaporate, without fanfare, without warning.

So much of life just slips away from us.

I didn't know the last time I rocked a child to sleep, the last time I received a colored picture from one of my children, the last time my son said he wanted to marry me, the last time I heard a child sing on stage, the last time I saw a daughter's softball pitch, the last time I saw my mother's smile. They all slipped away quietly, unassumingly, with me never suspecting the gravity of the moment. I also never knew my last mission trip to Mexico, the last time I sprinted or ate restaurant food without fear of sodium overload. And I never knew the last time I'd wake up carefree and not think instantly about my heart.

These soft endings were not endings until they were deemed so by future events.

Other endings are more expected. Your child's high school graduation is a door you see coming for eighteen years. Retirement, moving from a house, a daughter's wedding, my dad's last days battling cancer, all bittersweet moments that come at you with warning. These hard endings may be more difficult in the moment, but more easily accepted in the long run.

The soft endings, the unexpected ones, the ones that were not endings until the time had long past to appreciate them as such, are the tough ones for me. Life itself can be a soft ending. But like at an auction, I thought I'd hear "fair warning" before the gavel fell. Now I realize you usually can't count on that.

REMOVING REGRET

Our good God designed much of our existence as soft endings. He didn't want us obsessing over these very beautiful, but very human lasts. We can live captive to hard endings, which will always leave us bound to regret on the soft ones.

And regret can be a powerful force.

From my journal:

Heard some hard news today from doctors: My heart function is "abysmal," even for someone with heart failure. But that's not the worst part. Apparently, the heart is the only muscle that can't heal. It is one of the least renewable tissues in the body. Though meds and certain devices can help, the heart can't repair itself. So apparently, this is forever.

I have mountains of regret for not going to the doctor years ago when my husband first suspected something was wrong. Caught in its early stages, heart failure has a much better outcome. He urged me for years to get evaluated. I didn't want to be labeled a "hypochondriac." Now I felt more like the poster child for "Don't Be An Idiot."

I feel like I've failed my children and my family. I'd do anything for a do-over.

I had to move past that. And grace was my only way forward.

Early on, I learned that regret and grace can't be roommates.

My overdue diagnosis has taught me that grace is a big deal. Grace is the root of Christianity—if we can't embrace grace, we can't live in faith. For far too long, I wanted to believe in Him, and yet not accept that I needed His grace. Turns out, I was missing something big. As John Piper says, "Grace isn't just pardon, it's power."

Grace is God's perfect plan to bring all of His children home. But fully internalized, it is also a way of living this life until we get there.

Grace allows us to take risks with our faith and invest fully in imperfect people. And, perhaps most miraculously, it urges us past regret by extending God's costly pardon to ourselves.

We can't foresee soft endings. Eventually, everything we have here will disappear like morning fog, gone before your lunch hour. Meanwhile, we can only live as fully as this broken life allows. And rest in grace for the times we miss it.

Even when soft endings catch us off guard.

Especially when a sick heart (or a perfect dachshund puppy) is involved.

DAY 3

Home or Him?

Six countries, dozens of monuments, even more busses, trains, Ubers, taxis. Once we got approval for me to travel overseas, we hit the ground running—well, walking anyway. It would be trite to say it was the trip of a lifetime. It was the trip of a generation for my family. And I was thrilled to have all our children along for the journey.

Boarding our last flight from London to Chicago and then home, my black leggings were wrinkled and stained from eating and sleeping in too many airplane seats. I was out of clean underwear, out of low sodium bars, and out of energy. I was more than exhausted. We may have stayed a few days past reason this time, I thought to myself.

Still, in anticipation of home, even my failing heart would normally have an excited spark like waking up five years old on my birthday.

LONGING FOR HOME

I've always wished I were a morning person, a decent singer, someone with a little curl to my hair, and a lover of travel. But God in His perfect wisdom made me none of those.

For me, the best part of traveling is coming home.

But this time arriving home was different. I had left my children to board separate flights back to their own residences in different states. They were not with me on the last leg of the return journey. I wasn't yearning for home like I normally would. I felt something important missing.

Our longing for heaven might be the same, determined mostly by what we envision is waiting for us when we finally make it home to Him.

Early in the journey, we are comfortable here. But as we travel through this life, heaven becomes more alluring. Faithful friends and family die. We hurt daily, physically and emotionally. We long for the souls we miss and for the peaceful, pain-free existence we once had. The older we get, the more of what we desire slips to the other side.

The tipping point might be this: how much of what I want is on this side of eternity and how much of it now resides on the other.

HEAVEN'S HAPPINESS

I often wonder where my God figures into all of this.

Or if He even does.

Author John Piper begs a difficult question. "The critical question for our generation—and for every generation—is this: If you could have heaven, with no sickness, and with all the friends you ever had on earth, and all the food you ever liked, and all the leisure activities you ever enjoyed, and all the natural beauties you ever saw, all the physical pleasures you ever tasted, and no human conflict or any natural disasters, could you be satisfied with heaven, if Christ were not there?"

Could I be happy in heaven without Him? It hurt me to even consider the possibility. That I can imagine being content there without the One who made it all possible in the first place.

Finally home, finally at rest, but without Christ?

And then I realized that may be sort of a spiritual oxymoron. I don't think I would be there because I would have missed the point of this life entirely.

To be fair, we are mortal, and we cling to what we experience and remember. Home is often defined by the physical. Just like my own home being defined by my children being present.

It is difficult for us to imagine a home we have never seen that is defined by a God we know only by association. As C.S. Lewis wrote in

The Four Loves, "We are compelled to try to believe what we cannot yet feel, that God is our true beloved."

Our God is neither surprised nor wounded by this limitation. He understands our human nature, and His Spirit directed these words to demonstrate that. "We don't yet see things clearly. We're squinting in a fog, peering through a mist. But it won't be long before the weather clears and the sun shines bright! We'll see it all then, see it all as clearly as God sees us, knowing him directly just as he knows us!" (1 Corinthians 13:12 MSG).

ALIGNING OUR DESIRES

It's a difficult question to face. *Is the idea of heaven to complete our desires or to complete our God?*

Maybe it is to fully align the two.

Maybe it is to make God the complete desire of not only our afterlife but also of our current life. Skye Jethani, in his book *With*, urges us to seek an unending life with God, starting now. This may be the only way we can fully grasp the elusive concept of an eternal home.

After being released from the hospital the first time with my life vest, we finally came to the end of the 192-hour day that was supposed to include only a quick office visit. The next day I made the following journal entry:

I couldn't wait to be back home. I walked out the door for a doctor's appointment hoping to get an antibiotic over a week ago. I feel like I have aged twenty years since then. I left a bustling house full of family and I returned to an emptiness I have never known before. Children scattered to school and jobs. I completely missed the holiday.

As I stepped back inside the house, my life vest alarmed, to signal an impending shock to my heart. As if to say, "There's a new sheriff in town." I broke down in desperate tears, threw off the vest, and stepped away from it. Looking at that strange piece of equipment lying on my kitchen floor, I suddenly knew life was forever changed, for all of us.

Still, whatever happens next, I have this uncanny knowing that God is right in the middle of this. I can feel Him here, in what they say is an irreversible, unredeemable mess. His fingerprints are all over it. And somehow, even in the panic-riddled moments, that makes it okay.

As I breathed in the thick fear that day, the notion of home was palpable. I wasn't thinking about the bricks and the roof. And I knew I wasn't escaping my heart failure circumstances. My family was even gone. What I wanted was to be wrapped in the arms of a familiar God as I wrestled through the uncertainty and the heartbreak.

Finally, stripped of my expectations and plans, all I desired at that point was His full presence.

Whatever journey He takes this weary, travel-averse, doubting believer on. Whatever that might look like to get me home…to be finally, completely with Him.

DAY 4

Sinking into the Mud

Kansas heat can kill farm animals if they don't have water. It was a spoken truth my siblings and I all knew growing up. So, it was a big deal when, once I proved my dependability, I was given the job of watering the hogs twice a day during the summer. Everyone else was working in the field or in town. I was honored to have a job that carried so much weight, that Dad trusted me with (what I thought was) the fate of the entire farming operation.

Even with so much riding on it, I thought I had it completely under control. After all, I was about to be in fourth grade.

I would stroll the quarter mile down to the pens in tidy flip-flops, tank top, and matching shorts, dreading the large rude hogs. My goal was always to stay out of their filthy pen, to just drape the hose across the top of the tank, keeping it as simple and as clean as possible. Maybe even read a chapter book while the tank filled.

Approaching the pens one midafternoon, I noticed that the tank was not sitting level. The 200-gallon tank had an opening on one side to allow the hogs to drink from it. With the intense heat, the hogs had the ingenious idea to slosh the water from the opening with their snouts to make a mud bath. From the looks of things, they had been working on this plan for a while. Once the ground became soft from the mud, the tank lost its foundation and started to fall into the mud hole, emptying its cool contents onto the ground.

My dad's voice echoed in my head. *They can never run out of water in the summer or they will all die!* With no one at home, I knew it was up to me to resurrect their water source. I gritted my teeth and crawled into that pen. I strained to push the tank back upright, but my nine-year-old arms couldn't budge it. Worse yet, the 500-pound hogs were excited to have a visitor. The huge rough-skinned creatures ran toward me, snorting and squealing, pushing muddy snouts against bare legs as my toes and my flip-flops sank into the mud they had created.

BECOMING POWERLESS

I can still taste the tears of helplessness that overflowed into the pen that hot summer afternoon. The situation was bigger than any solution I had access to. When I realized it, whenever any of us realizes it, a feeling of powerlessness can set in.

Since my diagnosis, I have felt powerless many times. Often, I felt like it was a lack of faith, that I was somehow letting God down because I didn't believe enough that He could fix this. On worse days, I've felt like I wasn't doing enough to make it happen.

After months of meticulously titrating meds and completing cardiac rehab the first year of my heart failure, I was still hoping to avoid the internal device. I felt ready for another checkup in Cleveland. Although I seemed to always get bad news there, I believed this time would be different. I had committed to do everything in my power to get better.

I didn't know it then, but this would prove to be the low point on my graph of recovery.

From my journal at a checkup at the Cleveland Clinic:

Amazingly, in the huge city-like Cleveland Clinic, we got the same cardiac sonographer we had seen three months earlier. Evelina endeared herself to us right away because she asked to pray with us after my first echocardiogram. My husband and I were both convinced it was a good sign that we got her again. When we got back to the exam room, she said, "Do you remember me?" I said, "Of course! But how do you remember us? You must have done four or five hundred echoes since we've been here." She said she continued to think about us all the time and pray for us. She just couldn't get us off her mind; she felt like she had known us forever.

Once the echocardiogram started and the IV dye was administered, we started to get the feeling that it wasn't going well. Sonographers aren't allowed to reveal the results to patients, but it became evident anyway. Evelina got quiet, then asked if doctors were still talking about a transplant. I saw my husband put his head in his hands. She wanted to make it a tradition to pray for us. Then she said something that shattered our souls, "Are we still asking for healing?" My husband looked over at me in tears as our world stopped spinning.

Clearly, we weren't going to be living the vision we had hoped for, of dropping the Life Vest and walking out of that clinic mended. Not today anyway. Evelina gave me her personal cell number so I could keep her posted. She said she was expecting someday for me to be relaying a miracle to her. I wanted to believe it, but I wasn't so sure.

As we left the clinic that day, my heart sank, my hope sank, and my faith sank a little further into the mire. I had done everything in my power to fix this heart failure mess: fluid restriction, sodium restriction, maximum dosages on meds, sleep. Still, I slipped further into my illness, with no help in sight. And just like that little girl in the pigpen, I realized I was out of options on my own.

I didn't yet realize I was being incorporated into a story so much bigger than my own try-hard self could engineer, bigger even than my own improvement. Eventually, I found purpose there. As author and pastor David Platt noted, "I don't want to be a part of something that can be explained by my own ability or power. I want to be a part of something that can only be explained by the power of God."

THE AUTHOR'S POWER

Our good God had a plan, as He always does, and my mirky prognosis with heart failure was just one part of His great story. This low point turned out to be the high point, the point where I lowered my self-importance enough to let God step in. That day in Cleveland, I realized that my weakness, my inadequacy, is the ultimate qualification for serving God. It is God saying, "I choose you for this."

In choosing us, God often gives us more than we can humanly handle so we will lean on Him instead of our own imperfect power.

He knows we can become too intent on our own knowing, our own impact, our own significance in the story. But our God calls us to something more lasting, something more wonder-full. Be still and know. Be weak and wait. Be powerless and see.

Paul felt stuck many times. "We were under great pressure, far beyond our ability to endure" (2 Corinthians 1:8b NIV). Still, he leaned into his own helplessness. Later in the same book he wrote: "But he said to me, 'My grace is sufficient for you, for my power is made perfect in weakness'" (2 Corinthians 12:9 NIV).

God's power is evident most clearly in my own inadequacy. So the world may know. Because when I am out of options, it can only be Him being powerful.

That pigpen wasn't the last time powerlessness got the best of me, and it wasn't the last time I found myself sinking in mud. But it was one of the most memorable (and literal). I walked back from the pasture to the house that day, muddy and barefoot, but a little wiser. I was going home to make a long-distance call to Dad's office. Because of my dad's grace-filled parenting style, I've always known my Father was the One to turn to in crisis. And I knew He'd never scold me or demote me.

Those helpless days on the farm, just like my days trudging through the thick mire of heart failure, God wasn't waiting for me to do everything right. He wasn't waiting for me to check all the boxes.

He was waiting for me to be weak.

He was waiting for the moment my toes sank into the mud.

DAY 5

Learning to Lament

It was an ordinary Tuesday. As I slipped into the choir room ahead of the bell, I remember seeing her older brother pacing outside the school office, waiting for her to be released from class.

My childhood friend's mother had died after a long illness when we were seniors in high school.

I knew her mother was sick, but my world was spinning in a regular orbit, so I had never mentioned it. For years, I pretended not to notice her mother's decline when I spent the night enjoying her dad's culinary expertise, when I hung out in their upstairs TV room after school, or when I tagged along on their family vacations.

When I heard the news of her mother's passing, I didn't go to my friend's familiar house to console her. Her pain was something I couldn't understand and didn't want to see up close. Truth is, I felt a new kind of fearful sadness of my own that I didn't know how to express. So, I ignored it. I attended the funeral but pretty much expected everything to be back to baseline soon afterward. I'm not sure I ever talked about her mother's death to anyone, especially God, who had apparently dropped the ball. My friend and I tried to continue our normal teenage lives. Later that year, we graduated and went our separate ways. Before Facebook and at the height of long-distance charges, we drifted apart.

I put my God and my friend in a box marked "high school" and didn't take either one out for years.

I often wonder if it really was distance and decisions that came between us. I wonder how my relationship with God, and my friend, might have been different if I had expressed the unfamiliar disappointment, anger, disillusionment, fear.

Many of us eventually begin hurting in unexpected ways too. And most of us never articulate it. So, hard as we try to hold it together, grief seeps out in small drips and large downpours. It catches us off guard and spills over onto unsuspecting family members, supportive friends, and concerned co-workers.

God understands, and He wants us to talk about it.

God wants us to lament.

WHAT IS LAMENT

Lament is a passionate expression of grief or sorrow. It is more than just feeling the heartache. It is openly admitting to God the intense, confusing pain.

As humans, we suffer, but only as believers do we lament. And it is uniquely difficult because of the closeness of our God. We know His promises and we know Him. Yet, we live here in a world of sorrows, just as all His followers live, after the ascension and before His return. We live between promises.

And so, with feet in both worlds, a lament feels messy. We believe but we hurt, we know but we question.

Russ Ramsey in his book *Struck* describes lament as "a complaint bound to faith, confusion bound to trust, petition bound to allegiance." For the believer, grief seldom stands alone. It takes on a deeper dimension. A harsh reality hurts more coming from Someone we love and trust. In lament, betrayal mixes in with the grief.

From my journal the first year of my disease:

Nine months into this heart failure journey, I am wondering when God is going to step in. I am giving Him all the glory for holding this thing together so far. I know I should have never lived this long in my condition. But now, it seems like a logical next step, with me on so many prayer lists, to heal me and be done with it. I have learned to rely on Him and now it's time to display His love and power. But we are getting nowhere. No measurable improvement despite all the meds and all the interventions. When I vowed to never need the internal defibrillator, I was sure I was just claiming an early victory for God. Now it's scheduled to happen. I don't get it. Why not heal me, God? Why not demonstrate Your majesty? Why not move while people are watching? My healing after thousands of prayers and tons of faithful surrender seems to make perfect sense. I'm starting to feel duped or deserted—not sure which.

IN GOOD COMPANY

Both David, the man after God's own heart, and Jesus, the man who embodied God's own heart, were familiar with laments. Each cried out to God when his belief didn't seem to match his experience.

Jesus pleaded for answers in Gethsemane with the impending crucifixion, and at Golgotha in the middle of it. *I don't like where this journey with You is taking me.*

"[L]et this cup pass" (Matthew 26:39 ESV). *I want to pass.*

"[W]hy have you forsaken me?" (Matthew 27:46 ESV). *This hurts.*

David, dismissed, hunted, and rejected, penned nearly half the Psalms, and one third of those are laments: *How long? Why? Where are You?*

God's followers feel it in world problems, individual health crises, wayward children, lost jobs. Expressing our pain can sometimes feel disloyal, like we are giving up on God's ultimate goodness. Or maybe more like He's giving up on us.

But God intended it for something much different.

LAMENT DEMONSTRATES BELIEF

Lament shows belief like few other expressions can. In fact, it may be one of the truest forms of praise. Lament reaches out for Him when logic urges us to run away. Mark Vroegop says, "'The practice of lament is one of the most theologically informed things a person can do."

Psalms, Lamentations, Ecclesiastes, all focus on hurt and expressing it. They range from personal pain to shared suffering, and almost always end with a statement of confidence in the goodness of God, in praise. When we lament, we sift the truth out of difficult feelings and harsh realities.

Still, in the thick of pain, sometimes a lament feels like we are abandoning our faith. But it's just the opposite. Lament announces that even though we don't like what's happening, we're choosing to trust. When we lament, we are re-upping our belief in this God we don't understand.

I believe You exist. Just like I wouldn't send a letter or make a phone call to someone I didn't believe was real, by communicating to You I'm confirming that I know You are there.

I believe You are powerful. I can't hold someone accountable unless I believe they had the power to affect a different result. The fact that I am complaining to You means I know You could have done something about it. And that You can bring about a different result in the future.

I believe You love me. By sharing my deep personal feelings with You, I affirm that You are a caring listener. Otherwise, I'd keep the thoughts to myself. I hurt because I know You love me, and I can't humanly reconcile that love with my current reality.

Rather than suffocating it with silence, lament breathes life into our relationship with Him so no struggle is off limits. Passionate communication creates room for God, especially in our heartbreak. When we can be honest about our deepest pain, we allow Him in.

William Arnot writes, "When I weep, Christ enters by the openings which grief has made into my heart, and gently makes it all His own."

Now years voicing the harsh *why not?* has brought me to a place of faith I wouldn't have found in a quickly restored life. He gradually dug deep enough into my heart for me to learn this freeing reality: He is in control, and my shortsighted requests are not. I am finally leaning into that trust with commitment and even relief.

Whatever you're lamenting today, and we all are passionately grieving something in this remodeled world, don't be afraid to bring God into it. One day when we've walked farther on this sidewalk, we will realize even the losses were meant for more than we know.

When I found myself in unfamiliar pain over my heart diagnosis, I shared my questions and complaints about God online. My high school friend sent several messages of support. This friend also sensed how I was hurting because I couldn't be with my parents during their health struggles. Living nearby, she reached out to offer her help.

I know she understands my pain, and I see her decades-old hurt being used for good.

I just wish I had learned to lament all those years ago.

When my friend, and my faith, both needed it.

DAY 6

The Presence of Absence

After an unusually wet spring and a strong windstorm, a forty-foot oak tree fell in our front yard. It mercifully missed neighbors' houses and cars. It seemed to lay down perfectly, inches from disaster. We were able to find a tree trimmer nearby to cut it up and haul it away, and even grind the stump that same day.

To the neighbor walking her dog, or the occasional visitor from across town, it appears now as if it never existed. When they look at the front of the house, it is missing. But they don't know it. When I look at the front of the house, I feel an emptiness because it once stood proud and sturdy.

My heart aches in a way theirs cannot.

It's not just that something is not there. It was and now it's not. It is missing in a way that differentiates a hole from a blank space. Or the absence of a grand tree versus the decision to never have planted one. This unusual longing, this ache, has a special word for it.

It is *saudade*.

WHAT IS SAUDADE

Saudade is a term often found in the literature and music of Brazil and Portugal. Like many rich words, it has no English equivalent. This word came to life in the fifteenth century when Portuguese ships sailed to Africa and Asia in hopes of opening trade routes. Wives, children, and elderly parents who stayed behind suffered a strange sadness for those who departed into the unknown. Some voyagers disappeared in shipwrecks, others died in battle, many simply never returned. The family fragment shouldered a constant feeling that something big was missing from their lives, a yearning for the presence of the loved ones who had sailed.

Saudade has been described, perhaps best, as "the presence of absence."

It is more than something being missing or absent. Like the impression left in a lump of clay, it bears the distinct mark of something that was but no longer is. Saudade is the moment you realize how important people are in your life and the moments you have not fully lived with them. It is remembering your late husband or launched son, feeling the emptiness, and knowing nothing else can fill it.

Even more strangely, the absence is a presence in your soul that you treasure. As a wound that aches to remind you of something precious that is gone, you welcome the hurt to remember the joy.

A MYSTERIOUS MISSING

I have felt saudade for many things along my health journey: my energy, my security, the chance for the heavy cloud to lift even for a day, my ability to plan for the future. Others experience this longing for the distant and the unreachable with even heavier hearts: for children taken too young, for marriages lost to carelessness, for lives dissolved into poor decisions. We all know this mysterious missing.

The evidence of my saudade is not a physical hole or an empty imprint. It is a piece of hardware. A metal box protruding from my chest that threatens, at any time, to knock me off my feet to keep me alive. The subtle ache reminds me of what has been: the limitation-less life I once had. The presence of that box reminds me of the absence of my naïve security. But in classic saudade fashion, I welcome that ache. I do have a hole representing losses, as we all do. But without those craters, those rude potholes, we may have sped through life and missed the important scenes. The scenes where God shows up.

Just days before surgery to install my internal defibrillator, I wrote in my journal:

Reality of the surgery is setting in. I haven't begun to process this on so many levels:

1. *Surgery, by definition, hurts. I have a fear of flesh wounds.*
2. *I will have a foreign object in my body for the rest of my life, and it will stick out of my chest and be very visible so I will be reminded of that every day of my life.*
3. *This device is notorious for giving "inappropriate shocks," or going off when it doesn't need to. Nearly one third of people who get one develop anxiety disorder.*
4. *This is the last resort, as my doctor said, "the last card we have to play" before transplant. I'm scared more than anything that it won't help me.*

God did show up after surgery, and in a big way. My initial improvement was much grander than anyone anticipated. But it is not a cure. I still have heart failure, and my heart function still has peaks and valleys. I still have that hole and that dreaded device. The physical ache reminds me of what was lost, and some of it was for the better. I lost my security, but I found trust. I lost my wholeness, but I found a strange joy in the brokenness. I lost my carefully constructed future, but I found comfort in the one He's forming.

LOVE THAT REMAINS

A wise, anonymous writer called saudade, "the love that remains."

Despite the loss, regardless of the holes and amid the ache, the genuine love of saudade never leaves. Scripture would confirm the importance of this eternal feeling. "And now these three remain: faith, hope and love. But the greatest of these is love" (1 Corinthians 13:13 NIV).

We all suffer from saudade as we sail through this dangerous life and allow others to voyage on without us. The presence of the absence is both painful and comforting. Like the majestic oak or the grand life plan, we knew it once, we remember it, and we passionately miss it.

But as Christians, we know eternity has already begun, and when our existence takes a sharp turn at the edge of this life, we will fully know and experience the God who is love.

And only then will we finally have our saudade satisfied.

DAY 7

Survivor Guilt

There were three of us in our congregation desperately ill at the same time: Liz, Lora, and Lori. None of us saw our diagnosis coming. All of us thought we'd beat it when it did arrive. We are all believers. We all had hundreds of people praying for us. We all have husbands and children who need us.

I'm the only one left. And so often I ask, *Why?*

NO LOGIC, NO FAIRNESS

I certainly seemed the most dispensable one. After all, Lora had young children still to raise and nurture. Liz had growing grandchildren she was influencing and a husband whose health depended on her. My children are all adults, on their own. My family is healthy. But there is no logic in the result. There is no leveling factor.

Eugene Peterson is a faith giant to me. He translated The Message and has always spoken straight into my heart. He addressed this "fairness" aspect of faith. "One of the surprises as we get older is that we come to see that there is no real correlation between the amount of wrong we commit and the amount of pain we experience."

When I see Liz's and Lora's faithful families, I wonder what they think. *Are they happy for me to be alive, long past the doctors' prognosis? Or still angry at God, with me as a constant reminder?*

I felt almost ashamed comforting Lora's teenage daughter after she died. How strange it must all feel to them. I wasn't sure if I should even be there. A few months earlier, Liz's husband told me at her memorial service, "As sick as she was, she was still on her knees praying for you." I felt humbled and guilty that I did not always pray for Liz and Lora like I should have.

I choked up and left. The weight of "why" was too much for me to bear.

NO EXPLANATION

The big question haunted me. *If He does answer prayer, why doesn't He sometimes?* It is easier to believe in a God who can but hasn't yet, rather than a God who chooses not to. But as Job discovered in his afflictions, God doesn't explain himself.

As Sarah Clarkson notes, "Like Job, we are drawn into the strange, bleak landscape of God's seeming silence as we grapple with the kind of pain that could unravel us altogether."

To be fair, sometimes His silence is more a communication problem than a constructed punishment. He simply can't offer an explanation that we could comprehend.

We recently left our dog Pearl for three weeks with a sitter she didn't know. We had never left her anywhere that long before. I know she must have been confused, and depressed, and wondering if we were ever coming back. The entire time, I wished I could have explained it to her, to tell her that I made sure she would be okay, and that this isn't forever. But there was no way I could tell her in a way she would understand.

The understanding gap between us and God is even greater than the one between Pearl and me. And yet, we are intelligent enough to know we don't know, and it frustrates us.

NO REASON TO STOP BELIEVING

I remember planting a big garden on the farm. Dad plowed the ground and the kids followed with seeds to sprinkle in neat rows. Overseen and approved by Mom, the tiny flecks were covered and then marked by the seed packet so we'd remember what we planted. All planted in the same soil. All watered equally. All exposed to full sun. I never understood why some of the rows would have large gaps, or even entire rows empty, where the seeds never sprouted. I wanted an explanation, so we could be guaranteed 100 percent germination next spring. I never got that explanation, because there wasn't one to give. But this never meant we stopped planting anything at all.

That childhood memory has helped me come to terms with unfulfilled asks. Just because all of our prayers are not answered the way we'd like doesn't mean we stop praying altogether.

NOT ABOUT ME

I don't know why I was given more time, and Liz and Lora were not. It seems trite for me to say that God's ways are higher than our ways. Or that we're all here for different lengths of time, for unique purposes, none of us forever. And it's easy for me to say, because I drew the longer straw.

But from this perspective, I can tell you that answers are still unclear. Faith stills has a place, and I still struggle with God. From my journal the day after my first improvement in sixteen months, long after doctors had given up:

After a good long cry, lots of phone calls, a sleepless night recounting the entire ordeal in my head, and telling everyone that God had answered my prayer for improvement, something strange happened. Within twenty-four hours, I was confused and almost sad. How is this fair? I had a serious case of survivor guilt. How is it that this prayer was answered and so many others were not? What does it all mean?

Then I remembered Jesus' words about His friend. Months earlier, still in the thick of suffering, I had randomly opened to them in my Bible while visiting a new Bible class. The verse was underlined, without explanation and without my memory of it:

"This sickness will not end in death. No, it is for God's glory so that God's Son may be glorified through it" (John 11:4 NIV).

Lazarus wasn't healed so he could be immortal or to reward Lazarus for a job well done on earth. No, it was for God's glory so that God's Son may be glorified through it. My own healing was through me but not for me.

I am, as we all are, a very small part of a very large story. We never know what our chapter will include. But I know one thing for sure. One day, I will pray again for improvement, or for my life to be spared, whether from heart failure or something else, and God will eventually say no. Every person He cured eventually has died, even Lazarus. Can you imagine His friend praying to be saved from physical death, knowing that God had already resurrected him once? And how much it must have grieved God to say no?

Our God is a God of healing and restoration, sometimes here on Earth, but always in heaven. A medical cure here may grant us more years in this life, but not actually more time, because we have already been given eternal life. All of time belongs to believers. And whatever time we do have this side of heaven is for the purpose of glorifying God.

My sickness, and any incidental temporary improvement, have always been so God's Son could somehow be elevated through it. Tough assignment, but I intend to stretch toward that for the days I have left in this life.

Because I know that's how Liz and Lora lived theirs.

DAY 8

Waiting for Glory

Although the wedding far exceeded my expectations, I convinced my new husband to turn our tan Grand Prix around after we had made our confettied exit.

Something just didn't feel right.

I couldn't put my finger on it, but I reasoned it had something to do with not thanking my mother. Eager to get this marriage off on the right foot, my groom reluctantly agreed to drive back to the church. Back in I went, dragging my wedding gown train, amidst the cleanup, to hug my mother and my dad. I hesitated in that church fellowship hall for several minutes for my unsettled feeling to subside so I could begin my new life. But it never fully left me. And all along I knew it had nothing to do with the marriage itself.

I had all I had ever hoped for. And it wasn't enough.

A UNIVERSAL FEELING

It wasn't the last time I felt this heavy emptiness. It showed up again at holidays, during trips to Disney, even on mission trips. After the birth of each child, as friends suffered with postpartum depression, I basked in postpartum euphoria. But even in those strangely glorious weeks, I felt something important missing.

Mysteriously tugging on me at times of my greatest happiness.

When all my deepest prayers had been realized, I felt incomplete.

It was more than expectations exceeding reality.

It was more than garden-variety disappointment.

The feeling ran deeper.

In 1986, teacher Christa McAuliffe died in the Challenger explosion pursuing her dream while I sat in a college classroom pursuing mine. A few months later, reading Harold Kushner's new book, *When All You've Ever Wanted Isn't Enough*, I thought of McAuliffe and how she had her dream—sort of. I was disappointed because Kushner suggested living in the moment, creating good memories, taking risks. *Have a child, plant a tree, write a book.* Something still didn't sit right.

The weight continued tugging at me.

The following year we heard on our radios the new song from the band U2: "I Still Haven't Found What I'm Looking For," its gospel-inspired lyrics invading our Dodge Omnis, our dorm rooms, and our department stores. With tens of millions of YouTube views, Grammy nominations for Song of the Year and Record of the Year, and a place within The 500 Greatest Songs of All Time, there has to be something to this weight of universal emptiness.

AN INCONSOLABLE LONGING

Sehnsucht is a German word with no corresponding term in any other language. It is, like *saudade*, a profound spiritual longing. But it is an even more complicated phenomenon. Unlike saudade that highlights the absence and longing for something we once knew, sehnsucht is a longing for something we know nothing about.

In his famous sermon, "The Weight of Glory," C. S. Lewis acknowledged sehnsucht as an "inconsolable longing" for "we know not what." A haunting, indescribable desire, always pointing us to something beyond ourselves, beyond even this life.

"For our momentary, light affliction is producing for us an eternal weight of glory far beyond all comparison" (2 Corinthians 4:17, NASB).

Sehnsucht is the weight of glory, as we wait for Glory.

This weight of glory is to be connected to God and yet realize its inevitable incompleteness in this world. To be immensely happy and still missing the most important part of your soul.

Sehnsucht is finally having the very thing you had so desired and realizing that it was not what you truly wanted at all. That your soul longing involves so much more than you can plan or control or even comprehend.

"What no eye has seen, what no ear has heard, and what no human mind has conceived—the things God has prepared for those who love him" (1 Corinthians 2:9, NIV).

UNDERSTANDING THE EMPTINESS

Perhaps most vividly, I have felt this weight in my health journey. When all I had ever prayed for, all my prayer warriors had tirelessly petitioned for, wasn't enough. After my first unexplainable improvement, I had been called Cleveland Clinic's "miracle woman." But I had a heaviness inside of me. It felt odd and I felt guilty.

From my journal:

Sixteen months after being diagnosed with end stage heart failure, propped up by my device and a fistful of meds, my heart function has incredibly climbed into the low end of normal range. I should be ecstatic. But I'm still wondering why I don't feel anywhere near what I had expected. It is strange that everyone is so happy and I am holding back. What is wrong with me?

Doctors are shaking my hand and saying, "What a miracle!" It is nothing short of astounding that I am alive. I am grateful and in awe of the mountains that were moved on my behalf. And I never want to forget what happened and how it happened. I never want to seem unappreciative or unimpressed with that. It is huge.

Still, there is a pulling inside me that says I am still incomplete. I have nowhere near the capabilities, stamina, and longevity I had. And yet there is a distinct lack of anything to hope for now. Nothing left to pray for, nothing left to try, nothing left to save the day. There is a real possibility that this is as good as it will ever get.

Although my journal entry was about my health not being fully restored, in a sense, that's what we're all feeling in this life: not fully healed, not fully whole. The weight of glory tugging when all we've ever wanted isn't enough.

After searching decades for it, most intensely on the best days of my life, I have discovered something about this weight of glory.

Maybe the answer is not in trying to find it this side of eternity. But rather, in recognizing that we can't.

Maybe the weight was always meant to pull us home to Him.

And, at least for now, maybe the Glory exists in the weight itself.

DAY 9

Utility Room Faith

Functional rather than attractive, it never seemed odd or significant that we called it the "utility room" growing up. After a major remodel gobbled up our one-car garage, this tiny room became both a laundry room and miscellaneous storage. It was where our washer and dryer and muddy boots lived, and it is where my miniature dachshunds mostly lived too.

The days they weren't tied to the clothesline to guard their short, wandering legs from the path of farm trucks and machinery, I sequestered them in the utility room.

For practical, purposeful protection.

Even though I grew up on a sprawling Kansas wheat farm, I shrunk their world into twenty-four square feet. I did the same with other pets too. Rabbits forced into a tiny hutch, kittens shut in the small milkshed.

I've thought back many times on my consuming fear that my animals would die. Turns out, every single one of them did. Some even on the same road I tried to protect them from.

FEARING DEATH

Becoming a mother or a heart failure patient didn't do anything to quell this fear. Though I was sure I didn't leave a forwarding address, the familiar fear found me again in adulthood.

The New Testament writer was talking about me when pointing to those who "cower through life, scared to death of death" (Hebrews 2:15 MSG).

Something tells me the Spirit included this verse because He understands our struggle.

Death is inevitable, it feels final, and it feels unknown.

Perhaps it's where we've all been through the recent pandemic, trembling in a world filled with reminders of our own mortality. Jarring images of refrigerated trucks gathering bodies in New York City confirmed that even highly developed nations encounter unexpected, uncontrollable death. Our fear grew as the monster virus closed in on us.

According to some translations of the Bible, this fear of death can make us more like slaves. Even when our fear is warranted.

And often it's not just our own death we're cowering from. We could be constrained by the fear of losing someone we love, like my little dogs in the utility room.

Either way, we pull in and do anything we can to try to control that fear.

SHRINKING TO COPE

A doctor friend told me early in my heart failure diagnosis that the heart is the only muscle in the body that can't repair itself. Once damaged, it can compensate in other ways or rely on meds or mechanical devices, but it doesn't heal. Instead, it forms nonfunctioning scar tissue. Unlike bones that mend or tendons that self-repair, the heart doesn't produce new heart tissue. Once it's gone, it's gone. The heart can't regenerate.

When I learned that, I did a hard pull-back. I cowered. I wanted to believe I had half my life ahead of me and yet, my heart could never be what it was. It could only limp along. So, I set out to preserve the number of beats I had left. I lived short, eventless days to save up ticks of my heart.

I felt things go into slow motion in my life. I felt my days go from flourishing to something much smaller.

As I'm sure all my pets did, I soon learned that was dangerous and tight territory to set up permanent residence—for me and all those I love.

Months after suffering through his own case of Covid, my husband finally laced up his beloved running shoes, against my advice. As he did, I remembered his newly diagnosed mild aortic aneurysm, and I remembered the words of a favorite writer: "You're going to have to figure out how to live without knowing when you die." — Ann Voskamp

HE'S BEEN THERE

God understands our tendency to cower and shrink. His Book has plenty to say about fear and death. But even more than these worries, its pages overflow with unbridled hope.

And the most hopeful news is this: God is at His best when we are at our worst.

He is greatest when our own world seems smallest.

Throughout the book of Hebrews, the main message is Jesus is greater—greater than any tradition, any person, any fear. Even death. By breaking the power of death, He broke us out of our small, fearful world into His boundless realm of hope. This One who dove deep into death for us showed us we have nothing to fear.

"By embracing death, taking it into himself, he destroyed the Devil's hold on death and freed all who cower through life, scared to death of death" (Hebrews 2:15 MSG).

Still, Jesus did die, and most of His closest followers also died. He didn't set God's children free from the expectation of physical death, but from the fear of death.

Here's the catch: We can't be free from something if we've never felt bound by it.

So, it seems we can't be set free from fear if we don't first feel it.

FEELING THE FEAR

Even on their best days, my lively little dogs were clipped to a twenty-foot run of clothesline—my ingenious idea to allow them a measure of freedom during the day.

It was a feeble attempt to expand their world.

By the time I got home from school, the dogs could move merely inches. They inevitably wrapped themselves tightly and helplessly around the end poles. I never understood why they couldn't unwind themselves from that predicament.

We lived much of the pandemic, and even our lives, this same way. Wound up tight, running ourselves in circles to escape fear.

Fear of the virus.

Fear of life forever changing.

Fear of some things never changing.

But chronic illness has taught me something I couldn't see back in my pet-protecting period. Sometimes feeling that fear is just what we need…to remember to live.

From my journal:

Every time my heart lurches or has a spasm, every time my defibrillator alarm warns, I stop the busyness of life for that brief second. I put my hand over my failing heart, and I remember how short and unpredictable life can be. I remember the gift that it is. I remember the thin line we walk between the grocery store and eternity. I remember the people who will remember me. I remember to remember. That is the gift Jesus wanted for us at the Last Supper and when Noah was liberated from the ark to the fabulous rainbow and when the Israelites stacked rocks along the shores of the Jordan River. If we can remember, we can hold on to what we know about God and His short but sweet miracle that is human life. And we can move on while straddling the line this side of heaven.

Hope is a story we can't fully remember without recalling fear. By reframing this fear, by spending less time shrinking back in fear and more time feeling it, we remember to remember about our good God. And an even bigger transformation happens within us.

GETTING FREE

Admitting our powerlessness over death unleashes us from the fear of it.

Psychologists agree. Fear is instructive, and it points out hazards. That's never more true than when we're wrestling the fear of death.

When we open up to the fear and reality of dying, we are freed from the bondage of carrying the heavy unknown. Recognizing our inevitable death releases us to live rather than constantly preserve and protect. As we move from defense to offense, we shift our focus from escaping demise to encountering the Divine.

"On hard days and easier days, amid joy and pain, I've come to embrace mortality reminders as strange but good gifts. They can ground me as a mortal before God." — J. Todd Billings

But it's not an easy assignment. It takes deep hope and broken-in faith to know that the final state of our bodies will not be the measure of our lives. And in this realization, we are admitting that the narrative of God's Story is much larger than our own life's brief chapter.

Whether we live a few years or a dozen decades, we must view it all through a wide-angle lens. "Everyone comes naked from their mother's womb, and as everyone comes, so they depart" (Ecclesiastes 5:15a NIV).

THE REAL UTILITY

Besides the dogs, our farm utility room contained a closet full of hand tools and warm, worn coats. It held two pungent green trash cans and an aqua blue sink with a well-used bar of Lava soap in the corner. If you needed a can of WD-40, the ice cream freezer, or a clothespin, you could find it there.

Utility refers to something practical and useful. But my business degrees remind me that the concept of utility is also used to model worth or value.

That little space was handy for containing my dogs and farm essentials, but maybe there was more to its true value.

Maybe the real utility of that room is how it modeled the transformation of my faith, from one like that small pet prison, cowering and fearful of death, to one more complete.

A faith for real life, most days still more functional than attractive.
Yet now a faith unleashed and unconfined.
An expansive, fear-facing, death-accepting, hope-producing faith.

DAY 10

Holding Loosely

A few years ago, as Advent slipped into view, I began slowly dragging out a smattering of Christmas decor. While I was in the attic, I came across a page I had kept from a Christmas coloring book. A picture of the baby Jesus with His new parents under the star of Bethlehem, carefully colored by my three-year-old daughter and then adorned with a baby chick sticker. The chick seemed out of place, out of season, with Mary, Joseph, and the Christ child. But she always loved animals. And who knows? There might have been chickens in that manger.

Every time my daughter visited a petting zoo as a preschooler, she was first drawn to the baby chicks. I was always in fear. Not for my child, but for the tiny birds. I just knew she would either (1) hold the chicks too loosely, drop them to the ground, and give them brain damage, or (2) hold them too tightly and squish them.

Ninety-nine percent of the time, it was the second concern that proved more valid.

LOOSENING OUR GRIP

When we love and value something, it comes naturally to hold it closely, to try to protect it. We hold most tightly what we treasure most. But more often than not, our grip can ruin our treasure. Like that baby chick, or Halloween candy hoarded long past spring, we hold too tightly and they become worthless in the end.

But what we love deeply we can't completely let go either.

So, we must instead learn to hold it loosely. Sounds easier than it is.

From my journal after my second major decline in heart function, three years into my disease:

It seems the losses I've suffered have made me more intent on clenching, holding onto what I still have. I desperately want to trust the process, the outcome, but it all feels like it's slipping through my fingers at an accelerating rate. I'm afraid to even get an echocardiogram now, terrified of more declines. I think I'd rather just not know. I feel like the cat in the poster my sister had in our shared childhood room, claws dug into a knotted piece of rope: "When You Get to the End of Your Rope, Tie a Knot and Hang On."

Against our nature, God calls us to hold our blessings loosely, jobs, health, relationships, family, financial security. To unclench the white-knuckle grip on these things and cling tightly to Him. Hold everything (and everyone) else loosely.

No one knew more about this than Job. Job with his children and his property and his wealth, and then suddenly without. "The Lord gave and the Lord has taken away; may the name of the Lord be praised" (Job 1:21b NIV).

Job knew about loving deeply. He rose early every morning to offer sacrifices to God in case his children had sinned unknowingly. He always honored God. And I believe he could do so only by holding things loosely.

Job knew that God's glorious potential for a life can only sit in the palm of an unclenched hand. Honoring God requires that your hand remain open, even after the blessing. Because the blessings can never be allowed to replace our God or our God's all-knowing purpose.

And by loosening our grip, we acknowledge that God knows more and cares more for us (and our children) than we could ourselves. We're saying to our faith-proven Father, *I trust You more than I trust myself.*

REAL LIFE LETTING GO

My baby-chick-loving daughter grew up to attend college in Southern California, 1500 miles from home. Weeks before the discovery of her coloring page in the attic, I was scrolling through social media. I stopped on a post from her roommate, saying to pray for the victims of the shooting. I felt a canyon form, then widen, in my stomach. As quickly as my internet could churn, I started Googling for information.

The unthinkable unfolded on my computer screen and then on national news throughout the day. Thirteen people killed in a mass shooting, a young woman from my daughter's college among the victims at a popular student dance spot.

The tragedy took place only minutes from my daughter's off-campus apartment. It was one of the safest places to live in the US—until that day.

What was I to say to my girl so far away about something neither of us understood?

My momma heart did what momma hearts do, and it broke for my child. Just like our God does for us, we feel what our children feel, whether we choose to intervene or not. We bleed for them in an attempt to save them from this messy world.

I wanted nothing more than to hold her tight and keep her within my sight.

Just hours after my best effort to console her, she called to say she was under a mandatory evacuation order from her apartment due to a nearby wildfire. Still hurting from the earlier tragedy, we talked about what she should pack. I told her not to worry about every little thing. "Take what you might need for an overnight trip." I was sure they were evacuating the students out of an abundance of caution.

That's not the first time my parental instinct went awry. And I'm sure it won't be the last.

Later came pictures of her apartment complex surrounded by flames, firefighters running hoses to nearby hills, with the entire campus and city under fiery siege. Hundreds of memory-laden homes and hard-earned businesses gone. Unexpected, unprecedented, and unbelievable, even to those accustomed to Southern California wildfires.

I watched in disbelief as live news covered the students sheltering in place in the university library, flames visible from the building's windows. I spent several nights in bed with my phone, watching live helicopter reports of the disaster, tabulating the fire's containment, waiting for the next text or call from her.

As the nightmare week ended, my grown girl got off an airplane, walked through our front door and into my arms. I was keenly aware that another momma's girl did not. And that many other families that seemed as familiar as mine no longer had a front door to walk through.

When my daughter got home, she had the clothes she was wearing and an extra shirt. She couldn't wait to change out of the socks she'd had on for four days. Even still, as she said, she was best case scenario, one of the lucky ones.

HOLDING WITH AN OPEN HAND

That same little girl who learned to hold the chick loosely was learning to hold other things loosely as well. And, reading again the story of Job's catastrophic losses and unshakable faith, so was I.

After Thanksgiving, I sent her back to scorched Southern California. Only days later, classes were cancelled again and evacuations were ordered for mudslides and flooding. They warned about life-threatening debris flowing through the Santa Monica mountains that she drove daily to campus.

Instead of panicking, I had open hands and holding loosely on my mind. And I realized it applied to pretty much all of life.

Thumbing through my phone of photos of the fire, I found pictures of me holding and then letting go, of my parents' hands earlier that year. Knowing my eighty-three-year-old father would begin another round of radiation. And not knowing my eighty-three-year-old mother would renew her fight with debilitating pain. And I was reminded of my own out-of-control health situation.

As I recounted the details of my daughter's ordeal, I thought of a world of people facing hollow holidays without loved ones. Good friends and sisters who have buried children and husbands and lives they once knew. Thousands who have lost homes and security. Brutal holding and letting go rhythms. Pain I can't pretend to understand.

And I thought back to releasing my daughter from our final hug so she could get on that plane to return to college, post-tragedies. I had felt an intention to clench. But living had taught me to let her go. Because it is only in the letting go that we can receive the blessings God has in mind for us and for our children.

Unfathomable as it can be at times, open hands prepare us for the greater potential we might miss. As David Benham says, "God's not going to give you what's in His hand until you let go of what's in yours."

Because when we open our hands, we create space for Him.

BALANCING LOVE AND LETTING GO

Maybe all of life is about learning to let go, releasing our firm grip into a loose hold.

Advent helps us see what Job already knew, that deep love and holding loosely are the same thing. "For God so loved the world" (John 3:16 NIV) are Spirit-filled words from an Author who knows all about letting a Child go. By sending His perfect Son, God demonstrated this loosely held love and extended it to us. His holding love, tethered to each of us by the loose strands of free will. Boundless love forever guaranteed if we choose to make room for Him in our open hands.

God understands the careful balance that deep love and holding loosely require. I was starting to understand it in a larger context too.

Continuing to unpack our family Christmas ornaments, I opened a box of my favorite ones, those I had wrapped extra carefully. The plastic bubble wrap did not coexist well with the August attic heat. My treasures were ruined. The ones I had tried most intently to protect, I had lost. I smoothed the wrinkled coloring page with my daughter's carefully drawn name and unseasonal sticker on it. Tracing the crayon strokes, I prayed for her safety. And that she'd make it back home for Christmas.

I was relieved that I hadn't overprotected her unlikely masterpiece. That instead, I had held it loosely.

And I had a new appreciation for the sticker my wise three-year-old had chosen all those years ago. Maybe that little chick wasn't so out of place in the manger after all.

DAY 11

Anticipating Bad Days

I had planned and expected a really good day.

As I was just emerging from my painfully shy cocoon, my mother appliqued a dress for me. I loved everything about it: the careful hems, the shiny buttons, but mostly the Humpty Dumpty assembled from familiar bits of fabric on the front. It was a work of art and a rare treat. I felt my goal of becoming more popular coming into fruition. So, I saved it until just the right day to debut it to my third-grade classmates.

As Mrs. Voran's class lined up in alphabetical order for lunch that day, I peered down at the perfect stitches and the bright, winsome colors. I was sure everyone else saw it too. I basked in the glow of my wonderful day.

Until the unexpected happened just before I reached the lunch attendance secretary.

I had no idea the boy behind me wasn't feeling so well. Apparently, he held it together until the cafeteria smells got to him. Without warning, I felt a disgusting splash on the back of my dress, followed by expressions of further disgust by onlookers. Spinning around, I noticed the boy seemed to be feeling better, but my day had taken a sharp turn. Immediately, the teacher escorted me to the office where calls to my mother's landline went unanswered. A determined Mrs. Voran tried to use the stiff brown paper towels and the pink liquid soap in the girls' restroom to erase the evidence. We both knew it was a feeble attempt.

I returned to class encased in a feeling of humiliation, a damp dress, and a cacophony of smells. I suffered through the last three hours of school and a bus ride home until I could finally change clothes.

Not the good day I was anticipating when I scheduled that as "new dress day."

EXPECTING THE BEST

That was 1974. But my expectations haven't changed much, even all these years later.

Like my new dress, a new year holds promise of good days. And if you're like me, you expect the good days to be the rule rather than the exception.

Each January, the crisp, pristine pages of my carefully selected agenda planner are brimming with potential. I imagine it filled with surprise parties and encouraging medical reports, family vacations and great online sales. Despite my expectations, after decades of living, I know enough to know that along with blessings, tears will fall on those pages.

Which ones, I don't know.

But there will be heartache.

Because, although my agenda planner is new, my life is not. And He hasn't yet come to make our world new again either. So, I have the same worries, the same bills, the same disease.

With each new calendar, you sense this too.

And, like me, you've experienced it.

That day in third grade was a bad day for me.

But others, much worse, came later.

A freshman high school classmate died. My best friend's mother passed away after battling lupus. My own mother was diagnosed with breast cancer. A local seven-year-old boy suffocated in a farming accident. Divorce, hostages, financial devastation, tornadoes, car accidents. All became part of my known world before I graduated from high school.

And every single one took me by surprise, knocked the wind out of me, and left me questioning how God could let this happen. What makes bad days so hard is that we think of them as rare, as a glitch. So, they catch us off guard and they hurt more. Like a punch in the gut when we're relaxed.

ADJUSTING EXPECTATIONS

From my journal:

At my last visit to the Cleveland Clinic, my cardiologist told me, "You will be aware every day for the rest of your life that you have heart failure. You will have good days and bad days." She's right. Bad days are spent primarily on the sofa with a blanket and my dog Pearl. Although I wish those days didn't come, I am no longer surprised that they do. Though nothing has changed about my treatment or condition since my last downturn, I somehow feel so much better since she warned me about bad days. And I trust her even more because it matches my experience.

God told us this too.

Ecclesiastes is a strange (even cynical) book describing in detail a fallen world. Its inclusion in Scripture was fiercely debated for centuries. But I'm so thankful it made the cut. Its honesty has strengthened my faith in a trustworthy God. Because I've asked similar questions and I've experienced the same frustrations.

We spend most of our lives trying to protect ourselves and our family from bad days. But the truth is, they are coming anyway. God didn't say He would protect any of us from them. In fact, through Ecclesiastes, our faithful Father wanted us to understand just the opposite.

The rest of Scripture confirms this when we read it all right side up.

"For he makes his sun rise on the evil and on the good, and sends rain on the just and on the unjust" (Matthew 5:45b ESV).

"Shall we actually accept good from God but not accept adversity?" (Job 2:10b NASB).

"Even though I walk through the valley of the shadow of death" (Psalm 23:4a ESV).

In this broken, longing-for-heaven world, our story will contain bad days. No planning or prep will get us around that.

Even the Eternal Story reads this way.

It doesn't end with the peaceful baby in the manger. It ends with an empty tomb, by way of a really bloody Friday. If it weren't for the darkest day in human history, we wouldn't know the Glory, the day that absorbs all of our own bad days.

REDEFINING GOOD

Along the way, God wants us to understand that a *good* day actually has nothing to do with what's going on outside us. And everything to do with what's happening inside. Paul's prison prayers never contain pleas for changes in circumstances, but always focus on the heart of the sufferer. Paul knew a secret that countless other believers have discovered: That stained dress, that tattered situation, that devastating day, cannot reach a transformed heart.

After years of seeking a lasting physical renovation of my heart, something more miraculous and durable has happened: a spiritual renovation.

As Paul David Tripp says, "Be careful how you make sense of your life. What looks like a disaster may, in fact, be grace. What looks like the end may be the beginning. What looks hopeless may be God's instrument to give you real and lasting hope."

Maybe those inevitable bad days have been a tool to change hearts all along. To give us something permanent to cling to.

It's uncanny that the design on my dress was Humpty Dumpty. Because I felt like I was broken returning to my classroom. Silly as it seems now, I wasn't sure I'd ever be put back together again in my peers' eyes. I felt like a different person than when I left in that crisp, enviable frock. And I was. But not like I first thought. Ever since that cafeteria incident, I have paid more attention to other people's pain. And I have sought a more lasting security.

All of that happened on the inside because of what happened on the outside.

On a day I never would have planned.

God will call every one of us to exercise our mustard-seed faith along an impossible path in the coming year. On some pain-filled days. We can expect it.

That disappointing dress day, I started a lesson I'm still learning today: We should be making plans and resolutions that are very little about who we aspire to be on the outside and all about who God wants us to be on the inside.

And sometimes that takes living through some really bad days.

DAY 12

The Size of Loss

I am an ardent fan of trees, especially large old ones.

We searched for almost two years before we found a house with a yard full of mature oaks. My daughter was even married beneath their branches. It was my happy place.

But like grown children leaving the nest, they have gradually begun to disappear. Some trees are gone due to age, a few because of disease, still others following ice storms. Losing one every couple of years didn't seem to be that painful or noticeable.

Recently, five 100-foot oaks fell in our backyard and consumed at least as many smaller trees in their wake. The wet shallow root balls were no match for a strong August straight wind. One succumbed to the weight and then dominoed into the others. Collapsing one by one, our yard became a graveyard for trees older than anyone in my family.

It is a sobering, humbling scene.

I am reminded again of loss and how it can be swift and crushing and out of our control. Those mammoth horizontal trunks make me feel so small and powerless as they lay like slain dragons across our backyard. It seems as though the kingdom has fallen.

The devastation of the entire yard seems too much to take in. Right now, while we wait for overbooked tree crews to arrive, I am trying to look away. Pretending to not see the withering leaves and the craters from uprooted decades of growing. To protect myself from a loss I can do nothing to redeem. No money or skill or pleading could make it right again.

Even after the mess is finally cleaned up, nothing will seem quite the way it used to be.

THE COMPARISON TRAP

But in the middle of the hurt, I tell myself, *It's only trees. Thank God no one was injured. Others didn't fare so well.*

The same week a seven-year-old girl lies in a hospital in Wisconsin, with thousands praying her through a traumatic brain injury from a freak accident.

My daughter texts pictures of another Malibu fire she can see from her college campus. That community still shudders in the wake of the massive Woolsey fire that devoured 97,000 acres, 1500 structures, and three lives.

As I write this, a storm threatens to hit the east coast as a Category 4 hurricane. Dozens of cities scramble to prepare.

Funerals begin for victims of yet another shooting in Texas.

A family friend is battling through cancer with her husband for the second time. Another dear friend reimagines life without her husband lost to cancer a few months ago.

And I'm worried that my backyard is destroyed?

I have felt this comparison trap with others in my own illness. From my journal:

It continually amazes me that people with their own lives and worries and heartaches still pray for me every day. I can actually feel guilty about that. I have had my stint on the prayer list, and it should be time for someone newer, sicker, needier. Sometimes it is good to have the focus of attention off my health, but I can never take comfort in someone else's illness or life situation being worse than mine. Because I feel like I carry part of their worry in my heart as well. And that trap snaps both ways. Sometimes, after almost four years in heart failure, I think people are afraid to confide in me with their hurts because they think, "How can my concerns compare to hers?"

ANY LOSS IS SIGNIFICANT

Our loss can never be compensated by another's greater loss. And feeling our own loss doesn't discount someone else's pain. Because somehow we all share each loss. It's why mass shootings and childhood cancer hurt so much even when we don't know the victims.

Loss makes us all part of the same divine story in distinctive ways. Even when our loss seems humanly insignificant.

Scripture tells us who this Author is: a God who, rather than loving us from afar, always chooses to be part of the smallness of our lives. A God from whose care nothing escapes. A God who knows when a single sparrow falls from the sky, or when a single hair falls from my head.

Or when trees fall from my yard.

Jesus never said, *Qualify for My peace and grace by proving the size of your loss.* He said, "Come to me, *all* you who are weary and burdened, and I will give you rest" (Matthew 11:28 NIV, emphasis added).

He treated the wedding wine miracle with the same care and investment as He did in raising Jairus's daughter.

In Jesus's economy, there are no deductibles. All loss is significant and worth covering.

Because He knows that with any loss, it is more than the thing that is missing. It is memories of what was and plans of how life was supposed to be going forward. Like planting a tree, we expect it to always be there to provide shade and shelter and beauty.

EVEN TREES MATTER

My trees matter to God.

After all, trees have always had a main role in His story of loss and redemption.

They are mentioned in the Bible more than any living thing other than man and God Himself. As Matthew Sleeth noted in his book *Reforesting Faith*, every important event in the Bible was marked by a tree or some part of it: a branch, a seed, a bush, even a stump. Trees speak to us of our lives and our place in growing God's kingdom. A tree is a long-term project, like sharing faith. Hoping it takes root, hoping it provides refuge.

And both Eden's tree and Calvary's tree usher in the deep loss necessary for understanding the power of God through that faith.

God never asks us to ignore a loss. He never looks away, and we shouldn't either. Because in feeling the loss, in seeing the emptiness, we come to the understanding of our great need for Him, in all aspects of our lives.

So I will experience my loss and be different for it. I will be thankful for those who planted or preserved my trees all those years ago. I will commit to plant a tree that will take a century to grow. One that I can never see a child climb or a family rest beneath. Stepping into the future with a foot that will never touch its foreign soil, but with a shared faith that will help another on her loss-laden journey.

Whatever loss we're facing, even if it seems small in comparison to others, it's not small to Jesus. And we can know that our mighty God is already at work making everything new.

Recovering from all kinds of loss, we are each a unique part of His redemptive story.

Just like my yard will be for years to come.

DAY 13

What Lasts Forever

She was never meant to last forever.

But I didn't know it.

Growing up on our isolated farm, a door-to-door salesperson was a rare treat. So, my mother always welcomed in the Avon lady. Mom usually purchased practical items like lip balm, skin cream, or bath oil, but on a few memorable, yet ordinary days, I somehow managed to snag something special.

Like Petunia the Pig Soap-on-a-Rope.

I remember holding the pink egg-sized darling in my grateful hands. I marveled at her sweet chubby face and her just-right scent. I was moonstruck.

My older sister urged me for months to put Petunia in the tub with us. But I couldn't bear the thought of her melting away. I made a bed for her out of an old matchbox, tissues for sheets, and pledged to protect her forever.

But there was a glitch in that plan. The little rope tail fit perfectly over my preschool wrist. And the temptation to swing her around was too great. Petunia hit door frames and cabinets, TV consoles and fireplaces. When I first noticed how her ears were shrinking, her face was less defined, her snout not symmetrical, I was horrified. One evening, as we had our three-minute talk before going to sleep, Dad explained that she was just made of soap. He gently helped me understand this hard truth: it was not her purpose to be indestructible.

DESIGNED TO DISSOLVE

In my graduate business classes I later learned that Petunia was a *consumable.* Avon wanted us to buy another Petunia or her seasonal replacement in their next campaign, and the next, and the next.

She was never meant to last forever.

Actually, not much is.

It's been a brutal, lifelong lesson. I've clung to possessions, my kids' childhoods, accomplishments, my health, before I realized a simple truth: every world-bound thing, even our existence here, was designed to dissolve.

It took a chronic diagnosis and decades of living to figure it out. But I'm getting okay with it. From my journal:

After Dad's graveside service, we had lunch in the church basement for the family. It was good to be somewhere away from the house for even a short time. After we were all seated, I heard a strange low hum. Like I always do, I assumed it was coming from somewhere else. But it was my internal defibrillator preparing to shock me. My husband guided me into deep breaths and it stopped. Still, it was a dim reminder that we all have a date with death. The events of the last week had been overwhelming, and we were attributing the device issue to stress and lack of rest. So, when we got home, I laid down briefly. On the nightstand, I noticed a yellow notepad with Dad's scrawled handwriting. Now that he is gone, it is like finding a hero's valuable signature. He never had perfect penmanship, but his hand had been permanently curled for decades due to a botched surgery, requiring him to shake hands unconventionally, and alter his writing. Cancer had blurred his words even more. Dad was painstakingly recording symptoms, probably to mention at his next appointment: "stomach ache, tired—always want to sleep, brain fog, weak legs--especially ankles." Reading his pain, more tears were found, and I realized as much as I wanted him to still be with us, I could never ask him to come back here. His body was tired. It was time.

TWO THINGS ENDURE

Nothing here lasts forever.

We all know it on some level when we replace our roof or fill out the lifetime warranty claim on our ten-year-old Nalgene bottle, but most of us go about every day like we don't.

Jesus knew we'd need some reminders.

First teaching his followers:

"But store up for yourselves treasures in heaven, where moths and vermin do not destroy, and where thieves do not break in and steal" (Matthew 6:20 NIV).

As a believer, I have struggled all my life to live this in real time. Then I connected it to a later verse (not surprisingly addressed to Pharisees):

"'Love the Lord your God with all your heart and with all your soul and with all your mind.' This is the first and greatest commandment. And the second is like it: 'Love your neighbor as yourself.' All the Law and the Prophets hang on these two commandments" (Matthew 22: 37–40 NIV).

Deep into middle age, it was an *aha* moment for me when these two verses converged: When Jesus talked about storing up treasures and about loving God and your neighbor, he was saying the same thing. Because God and the souls of others are all that will endure into eternity. Nothing else is sturdy enough to last into forever.

Especially not these accident-prone, disease-harboring, wasting-away bodies.

Like that soap-on-a-rope, the physical *us* was never meant to last indefinitely.

FINITE BUT ALSO INFINITE

The glorious paradox is this: just as surely as we are finite, we are also infinite. We will live forever somewhere. So that use-by date stamped on our foreheads is a form of God's mercy. And a call to invest in eternity by buying into Him and others.

God promises that nothing I do to empower a soul for the sake of eternity will ever be wasted. It will be worth any temporary sacrifice I make. Because it sets our feet in forever.

This is the stuff of eternity.

Another rare treat we had growing up—chocolate candy bars. If one of us just happened to be alone with Dad in the right place at the right time, he'd buy us a Snickers or a Hershey's or a Heath. And we'd eat every bit of it before we pulled into the driveway at home. Dad knew how to invest in the souls of others.

One of my treasured comments after Dad passed was how in his public accounting business he had undercharged or even worked for free for clients that he felt couldn't pay (after all, he did know their financial situation). Facing cancer, he had every reason to be storing up funds for his medical treatment and other costs. But he stored up a different kind. As the beneficiary of his three-minute nighttime talks, it didn't surprise me much.

John Piper advises, "Life is short. Eternity is long. Live like it."

I think Dad would agree. *Take the trip. Make the phone call. Burn the candle. Use the soap. Eat the chocolate.* But most importantly, *love the person in front of you.*

When my parents moved off the farm, I helped them pack a few boxes (way less than my share). Much of my childhood room was still intact. Going through my desk drawer, I found Petunia. She didn't age well. In addition to the injuries she had sustained from being swung around my wrist, she was cracked, dusty, out of style (sounds too familiar), and her delicate floral fragrance had vanished decades ago.

Thank God we have the reminders. Like Dad's note and that soap fragment. Those moments we briefly stop the spin and start to savor. Those moments we invest in the souls of others. Those moments when we realize we don't want this life to last forever.

Better is coming.

Look past the everyday to eternity.

You (and that soul sitting beside you) were made to last forever.

A Question of Doubt

Days 14–26

• • • • •

Jesus's Desert Dilemma

"'If you are the Son of God,' he [the tempter] said, 'throw yourself down. For it is written: 'He will command his angels concerning you, and they will lift you up in their hands, so that you will not strike your foot against a stone'" (Matthew 4:6 NIV).

What We Hear

If I am God's child, He won't let me be harmed.

Life Question

Is God always good?

DAY 14

Surviving a Collapse

For nearly a decade, my mother and I shared a twice-yearly tradition/obsession.

We met in a small town between us for their semi-annual citywide sale called Crazy Days. We woke before dawn to beat other bargain hunters to the mall or the gift shop or the local boutique. Both of us owned furniture and coats we didn't need but that were too great a deal to pass up.

I later learned it was one of her favorite memories. And mine.

Except for one incident.

One early August morning, we arrived as mall security turned the key in the lock. We had staked out the territory the night before, so we knew where we were heading—the upscale department store on the end. As we walked through the doors, I felt giddy at the 90 percent-off opportunities. I glanced over at Mom just in time to see her starting to stagger. She walked into a rack of clearance clothes and collapsed.

A mini-emergency ensued. Mom was unconscious. With no cell phones, store clerks and I tried to figure out what to do next. I was scared, my mind was spinning. We were both hours from home. Eight months pregnant with my first child, my immediate thought was *I can't navigate the scary next years without her.*

Barely twenty-six, I couldn't imagine a life after that kind of collapse.

TYPES OF COLLAPSE

The news is often full of different kinds of collapse: health care systems, the stock market, international governments. Others are more physical: poorly built buildings, hurricane- or flood- or wildfire-ravaged neighborhoods.

One clear afternoon, the new sunroom on my next-door neighbor's house collapsed during a re-roof. Under the weight of the new shingle stacks, it just fell in. Broken windows and twisted metal everywhere. We stood in shock as we took in the ruin from our adjacent yard.

Most collapses catch us by surprise, like the disaster next door or Mom's fainting episode. Others we fear but never happen. Remember the Y2K computer scare that was supposed to bring down the world's infrastructure?

Any kind of collapse can be traumatic. But the worst is a spiritual one. It happens when we can no longer reconcile what we're experiencing with what we believe. It happened to me. The fault lines and weak fittings of my faith were revealed. Life started to collapse, and I felt powerless to prevent it.

From my journal the first week of my diagnosis:

The cardiac nurse practitioner had introduced herself the day before as I was being admitted to the hospital and undergoing tests. Today, she walked solemnly into my room saying, "I'm about to pull the rug out from under you." I didn't know what else she was going to say, but I felt the seriousness. She stood at the end of my hospital bed, gripping my ankle through the bedsheet as if to brace me. I had known her for 24 hours, yet she had sympathetic tears in her eyes. I felt my chest caving in. "Heart failure" echoed in my ICU room and down the hall and all the way back to the secure home I had left.

CAUSES OF COLLAPSE

Physical collapses can be blamed on construction, corrosion, or cracking. A force of evil or a force of nature. It's not much different for our lives in general.

(Mom's collapse turned out to be low blood sugar. In our haste to the mall, we had skipped breakfast. My health collapse, undiagnosed for years, has been attributed to a virus.)

Our carefully built every day can survive until it must bear a heavy burden: loss, illness, disappointment. Then what supports it is revealed. If that support is faulty, our world can collapse.

"Everyone who hears my teaching and applies it to his life can be compared to a wise man who built his house on an unshakeable foundation" (Matthew 7:24 TPT).

These were Jesus's words, but as we live them off-paper, in real-time, it gets confusing. Like His entire Sermon on the Mount, they seem to represent some unfulfilled promises in my life.

After my diagnosis, I ransacked the Scriptures for answers and realized we all carry some translation of this construction story. And I realized I may have held a faulty assumption. Jesus's teaching couldn't mean we are protected from the collapse itself. Every major player in the Bible went through some sort of devastation.

When Solomon's temple and its treasures were destroyed under a cranky king or when the cross came down holding the Savior's lifeless body.

When the whole world flooded or when Job's whole world did.

We all know that even well-built structures sometimes collapse. We've seen it with tornadoes and terror attacks. No matter how we try, the force of this fallen world can tear down what we've built. Even what we've built in faith.

THE FOUNDATION REMAINS

Something I've noticed in all types of collapses—in the aftermath, what's left is only the foundation. The solid part. And in those laying down times, we begin to rely on Him.

As one chronic pain sufferer has experienced:

"This is my hope…that when I have lost everything that makes me who I am, I will still remain, because I am held up by something more solid than myself, than my body, than my very consciousness. I am held up by a love as strong as death." —Liuan Huska

This foundation is God's safety net. And maybe that's what Jesus was saying in His Sermon after all. The Beatitudes describe several collapses that always end in God's care. When it feels like all is gone, you can only fall so far. He never promised it won't be painful, but He did promise a threshold in the Father's arms.

What my cardiac nurse practitioner didn't know, and I didn't either as plans were crashing and futures were shattering, is that even when the decorative rug was pulled out from under me, there was something underneath that would keep me from falling too far. Though I didn't see it for months, when the walls of the familiar fell in, the foundation remained.

It's often not until what we've built has collapsed and the debris is cleared that we notice the solid foundation that has been holding us all along.

A PLACE TO REBUILD

The foundation gives us a base to start rebuilding. It allows us the opportunity to pick up the pieces and start again. My neighbor is putting up a new sunroom on the same concrete slab. A re-imagined version on the exact site of the original one.

After "God with us" Jesus left the earth, "God in us" Spirit arrived on His same footprint. Job's solid faith allowed him to begin reconstructing a life post-tragedy too. The same thing happened with the temple.

"[L]et its foundations be retained" (Ezra 6:3d ESV).

Built precisely at the place of the first one, the restored temple marked a fresh start—the renewal of Jewish life after the devastation of exile. It signaled a new role for the people themselves as builders. And the second temple would occupy a greater place in Judean life than Solomon's temple ever did.

Every collapse clears the site for what's next and gives us a place to start looking at a blueprint again. After all, as author Katherine Wolfe says, "We're all living some version of a second chance."

There would be other family collapses in the thirty years that followed that mall incident: a string of unexpected early deaths, clusters of financial hurts, numerous health crises, scattered life disappointments. But somehow, we always survived. Even when all that was left was the foundation. We only fell so far.

I lost both Mom and Dad within four months, and I felt no more ready for that collapse than I was that crazy day at the mall. But now I can clearly see the faith foundation they laid for me.

And, with my heart failure stable and life plans starting to reemerge, I feel ready to begin building again.

DAY 15

A Prodigal's Parent

It's one of my favorite Dad stories.

Driving home from college for Thanksgiving, my dad and his buddy got stuck in a snowstorm. The inexperienced teens should never have been on the roads. Without cell phones and with limited emergency services in 1951, the three days they spent in the car, turning the engine on every few hours for warmth, created a catastrophe at home. My grandma wondered if she'd ever see her only son again. She would have done anything to get her boy home. I imagine her scanning the horizon constantly, waiting for the sight of his car crawling up the snow-packed driveway.

A PARENT'S PERSPECTIVE

This tidbit of family history conjures up thoughts of the Prodigal Son. As in all of Jesus's parables, that son is every one of us, an overconfident child naively and frivolously spending a life and an inheritance. And ultimately just looking for a way to go home.

Most of my life, I have identified with the lost child in this story. As prodigals, we shoulder a certain regret: we have disappointed our parents, disappointed our God, disappointed ourselves. But sometimes we focus too much on what we have done or failed to do and our own importance in the story.

Perhaps all along, the story, our story, has been much more about what He does and very little about what we do. Maybe it was always meant to be about the Father.

Travel-wise I grew up in a different time. When the world existed only on one side of the globe. And while troops and products crossed the oceans, people didn't. In fact, when I left my Kansas home to attend Oklahoma State University, I thought I was studying abroad. For me, for my dad, and especially for the prodigal son in the Bible, families stayed close and worked on living and surviving. So, when that boy in the parable left his dad for the far country, it was likely a family crisis.

This got me thinking about that prodigal's parent.

WANTING US ALL HOME

Like the parent in the parable, I have felt the two-way tension in my children's ties to home. Wanting them to come, but more importantly, wanting them to want to come. God, the perfect Parent, wants that too.

And His story carries the theme throughout.

Max Lucado writes, "Christmas begins what Easter celebrates."

While Advent is the first baby-soft whisper of God's invitation home, Lent calls to us in a more mature voice. Beckoning us back from a difficult journey, home to God, where we are loved and safe. Back with the God whose arms are fully open. Into the embrace of a God who runs toward us. Even in our sin. Especially in our shame.

Lent reminds us that because of the resurrection, our good God continually searches the horizon for His prodigal. Hoping for us to want Him. Hoping for us to walk toward home.

"For this son of mine was dead and is alive again; he was lost and is found" (Luke 15:24 NIV).

Just as Jesus came to reveal the Father, Lent gives us a glimpse into the heart of the prodigal's Parent. He could never have seen us from a distance unless He had been intently waiting and expecting. And He would have never been looking in the first place unless He desperately wanted us home.

A MESSY REUNION

While we were visiting a city in another state, I lost my three-year-old son in Target. My eyes left him in the toy aisle for mere seconds and he vanished. A frantic search culminated with the heavy, grave sound of the front doors locking as they announced a "Code Adam." Blood froze in every vein in my body as I prayed for him to be on my side of the locks. I ran up and down every aisle calling his name, scanning for a little guy in a striped ball cap. All I wanted was that boy back with me. Nothing he had done or hadn't done mattered. And I never quit looking for him until I saw him being escorted to the front by a gray-haired woman.

True to the Bible's overarching theme of exile and homecoming, the prodigal parable is the saga of the entire human race. But perhaps most importantly, it is the story of God's long-suffering, His patient plan to bring us all home. Jesus took on the ultimate exile in death so every one of us could find our way back to the Father.

And He did this while we were still figuring it all out. Not after we were sinners, but during, in the ugly, messy middle of our rebellion and distrust and uncertainty. While we were still finding our way home. While we were still a long way off.

"But while he was still a long way off, his father saw him and was filled with compassion for him" (Luke 15:20b NIV).

ANTICIPATING OUR RETURN

From my journal the first year of my diagnosis:

We have a special sonographer at Cleveland Clinic, Evelina. It is a God-thing in this massive campus that we draw her each time to do our echocardiogram, the test that determines how well I'm really doing. From the very first time we came here, she quietly shut the door, took our hands and prayed with us. Somehow, she can sense that every desperate test outcome drives another wedge between me and God. And this time will be no different as we see in her face the poor results and hear in her prayer what she cannot tell us directly. "Please, God, heal Mrs. Lori's heart. I know this is the top heart hospital, but you are the top doctor and we trust you in all things." As if she were on a mission to make sure this didn't consume my faith. I am almost old enough to be her mother. And yet, in many ways, she is mine right now.

At that moment through the words of this medical professional, God was already anticipating my journey back to Him, just as the Father did in the parable.

So, if you've had trouble finding home because of misguided choices, naïve rebellion, or the circumstances of life, know where He is.

While you are still a long way off . . .

He is keeping vigil at the 1950s farmhouse window.

He is running through the aisles of Target.

He is holding your hand as the test results come in.

He is continually scanning the horizon, waiting for His child to come home.

DAY 16

What Love Looks Like

I was in fifth grade before I knew that a human heart is not smooth and simple and symmetrical. A trip to the science museum proved it. Wondrous and vital as the human heart is, it's also scary looking, lopsided, and a bit complicated.

Love first masquerades as a soft romance too. But when we see it from the far side of life, light is cast on a different angle, a bit messy, unpredictable, even harsh.

NOT WHAT I THOUGHT

As we hoisted Dad from his wheelchair into bed for the night, surrounded by pain-relieving meds, an oxygen tank, and bars of dark chocolate for comfort, he said, "That's the first time I've cried in fifty years."

My mother would not be sleeping beside him that night. Earlier that Father's Day evening, she had nearly died in a choking accident. She was in the local hospital, recovering from what had been a harrowing experience for all of us. But no one was more traumatized than my dad, watching his wife struggling to breathe, getting CPR, and being physically unable to help her.

Mom's words just after she arrived in the ER by ambulance: "I have to go home."

Dad's surprisingly sentimental words from his home hospice bed that same night: "She's the only girl I ever loved."

I smiled, figuring life's fragility and cancer's suffering had mellowed him. He had always seemed to me a man of few emotions because they didn't always look like I expected. For years, I carried in my wallet a note Dad handed me just before walking me down the aisle: *You will always be my baby girl. I should have said this many times before, but I always figured I didn't need to—But just in case, I Love You. Dad*

I've felt it every day but I treasure these rich, rare words.

Growing up, I had always hoped my parents would show their affection more like Michael and Carol Brady of *The Brady Bunch* or Charles and Caroline Ingalls from *Little House on the Prairie.* But I'm learning that might not actually be what love looks like.

It took me half a lifetime to see it clearly.

My parents' love, like God's, was something much bigger.

SOMETHING BIGGER

As my feisty mother pushed to be released, she walked the entire length of the hospital hallway her first time out of bed to prove she was strong enough to go home. Although outwardly she was indicating Dad wasn't that critical, inside she knew she had to get back to him. With her husband on hospice care, four days apart was a big deal.

After she made it home, Mom talked tough to Dad, trying to prod him to hang on, and shelter her own heart from the impending loss. I instantly reverted back to my six-year-old self, witnessing their familiar banter. A ninty-eight-pound drill sergeant urging him to use his muscles, Mom also fed him every bit of shrimp from her own Chinese takeout.

As I suppose most children do, all my life I underestimated my parents' relationship because I had one idea of what love looks like. Because they didn't verbalize it in front of other people or because they didn't lavish each other with expensive gifts or exotic trips.

Here's what they've shown me love really looks like:

Gumption to honor the covenant when your path takes a detour.

Grit when you don't like each other and life keeps slapping you in the face.

Grace through the letting go of dreams and grudges, children and parents.

God's word has a special term for that.

Hesed (or *khesed*) may be the richest word in the Hebrew scriptures. One of the most common descriptors of God Himself, it is found nearly 250 times in the Old Testament.

"God, *who is* compassionate and gracious, *slow to anger,* and abounding with loyal love and faithfulness" (Exodus 34:6b, LEB).

Hesed is the Hebrew word translated here as "loyal love." But the fullness of hesed cannot be adequately translated into any other language's single word or phrase. It's a special kind of loyalty—active promise-keeping loyalty demonstrated by deep personal care.

My parents had likely never heard of hesed, but they lived it daily.

Hesed is my mother carefully preparing Dad's favorite meals, even when he could barely eat during his years of chemo treatments.

Hesed is my dad printing emails and articles in large font for Mom every week since she never learned to use the internet and macular degeneration compromised her sight.

It is Ruth gleaning in unfamiliar fields to feed her widowed mother-in-law.

It is David showing loyalty to Jonathan's dangerous family.

It is God providing manna in the desert and, ultimately, Jesus on a cross.

All within a long-lasting covenant relationship.

It is commitment, choice, desire, and action…all rolled into one.

LIVING IN LOYAL LOVE

As impressive as it is, hesed is often not pretty at all.

This special brand of loyal love requires constantly getting our hands dirty—helping aging parents, changing new babies, directing stubborn teens, following the way of the cross. Hesed will one day compel us to do what wc never expected to do when we first drew parameters around the idea of smooth, simple love.

Like helping your cancer-stricken dad onto the bedside commode for the fifteenth time in the same night.

Like listening to his mumbled story with full attention and wonder for the fifth time in the same day.

Like falling asleep holding his hand while his wife is in the hospital and he says, "You can't leave me alone."

But mostly, hesed looks like your husband doing all of that for your father going on forty-eight hours with no sleep because your own health won't allow you to keep doing it yourself. For this rare son-in-law, Dad's passing was like losing a father twice.

The only way to show loyal love is in this continuing stream of everyday commitment. Hesed is a never-going-to-leave-you kind of love. Like God showed from Eden to Calvary. Like my parents did for over six decades, even when I didn't always see it.

While other love words in the Bible focus on feeling, hesed gets its meaning from action.

Mom's favorite quote came from Mother Teresa: "Do small things with great love." The key to loyal love is small things, constant things, vital things. My parents both knew about those. And their lives knit a safety net for me.

"The totality of your behavior will set a template of what love is that your children will carry with them into adulthood." —Neil Strauss

In many ways, my parents' example of hesed has helped me hold onto my faith through the harsh journey of heart failure.

Most of us have seen our lives not track the way we'd hoped and planned. (I saw my parents' lives take some unwanted turns.) Detours can make us into doubters. When this happened to me, I started to question if this God I had known and trusted all my life had ever really loved me at all. If I'm being honest, I questioned God's loyalty. But something deep inside me helped it make sense. From my journal:

If I embrace God's long-term character, through the good and bad isolated events in my life, I can see Him more clearly. Maybe I was wrong. Maybe God's love doesn't mean cleanly wiping this disease away. Maybe it means trusting Him in small things, even when He doesn't move big

mountains. Maybe it means Him loyally holding my disappointment and walking into an unplanned, even dim, future with me.

We often blame God for what happens on His watch. *Is this what love looks like? If it is, I may have to pass.* Maybe I've been guilty of holding both my parents and my God to the wrong standard. To the smooth, symmetrical, cookie-cutter kind of love instead of what love really looks like. Maybe all my life I've underestimated the impact of small, consistent, messy acts of loyal love. Maybe all my life I've overlooked hesed.

As the funeral home director wheeled Dad's body from the house, Mom leaned over, removed his glasses, smoothed his signature unruly hair, kissed him, and whispered, "I'll always love you."

And I finally understood what she meant.

DAY 17

Adjusting the Font Size

A few years ago, pre-heart-failure, I took my first trip outside this continent, a trip to Buenos Aries, Argentina, to visit our son who was studying abroad. Arriving with limited expectations and little savvy, we somehow stumbled into booking a trip to Iguazu Falls. I had never heard of it, but learned it is one of the New Seven Wonders of Nature.

Three times wider and one hundred feet taller than Niagara, Iguazu was impressive to behold. My husband and I both teared up seeing it. Then against the spray of the massive waterfall, a rainbow formed. The kids still remember "how weird Mom and Dad were acting." I honestly felt like I was witnessing a flourish of God's miraculous hand that day. I had a glimpse of Eden.

But honestly, most of my life, I haven't noticed God working. I knew Him and I loved Him, but I couldn't see that He was actually doing much in the miracle field.

SEEING THE SMALL PRINT

Turns out the problem was with the observer and not with God.

C.S. Lewis said, "Miracles, in fact, are a retelling in small letters of the very same story which is written across the whole world in letters too large for some of us to see."

My difficulty was with the smaller letters. I could see God in nature and in the resurrection, but I had trouble finding Him in my own life, or in the situations of those I love.

Thankfully, most doctors can see those smaller retellings. Seventy-five percent of US doctors believe miracles occur today. Let that sink in. The people who devote their lives to saving people realize that they are not the ones doing the saving. Something else is going on that they can't explain scientifically.

I recorded in my journal after an early trip to the Cleveland Clinic:

As we sit here, I can see clearly the front entrance of the hospital. Five lanes of cars bumper to bumper, dozens of CC employees directing traffic in the shadow of a six-story parking lot. This place is like a city unto itself. So very many souls seeking a miracle today.

Shortly after that, my appointments began. I had my first echocardiogram with Evelina, who would eventually become our favorite sonographer at the Cleveland Clinic. After she saw the test results, she prayed "for a miracle to heal Mrs. Lori's heart." Maybe for the first time I realized the seriousness of my situation. I'll never forget her words because she so clearly believed two things. One, I was desperately ill. Two, God, and only God, could fix this. She asked for a miracle because, with all her medical expertise and experience, she knew, more than anyone, I needed one.

Since that day, I have beaten all the odds and even the most optimistic predictions. I have survived and improved beyond medical explanation. To be clear, although my life was spared initially, my heart is not healed. I am managed extremely well with my device and medications. But I have a disease that takes one course, and it is forward.

Still, something notable happened here. God amazed the doctors and astounded the surgeons at the best heart hospital in the nation, perhaps the world. There is no denying that fact. And maybe getting heart failure in the first place, against any rational explanation, was somehow part of His miraculous plan.

Yet, even with this amazing experience, I get weary. And teary. Many days I still look for Him and go to bed disappointed. As we journey in this still-broken world, it can sometimes seem that we are on our own to tread the floodwaters of our situation for as long as we can.

GOD'S BIG PROMISE

Even Jesus saw some harsh happenings through tears. I often think Jesus wept at the death of Lazarus because He knew we'd be left to live in a world that is still not as it should be. And He understood that His Father won't always fix it.

We all know that God seems not to intervene at times of our greatest need. Those days when we can only perceive our circumstance through helplessness, we are perhaps experiencing our situation in its truest form. Seeing this world through the refraction of our human tears allows for the rainbows to take shape in our own lives. And those rainbows are promises.

"Never again will all life be destroyed by the waters of a flood; never again will there be a flood to destroy the earth" (Genesis 9:11b NIV).

God's promise throughout history has been this:

Even though I don't always rescue you from facing a flood,

I'll never again let a storm destroy all of life.

Or all of your life.

Just before my heart function was initially restored, my husband and I drove past our church building. Minutes before, we had been caught in a spring rain. As we approached the building, we noticed a rainbow and stopped. Then we saw the complete arc, with the church building sitting perfectly centered underneath. I knew then that the deluge of this disease will not ruin me. Whatever the outcome. About a week later I wrote in my journal:

I remembered today about the rainbow I photographed three days before we got the news of unexpected improvement. I had never been able to see both ends of a rainbow that distinctly. I feel like God was sending a message that I would one day see this journey completed. I just may not know how or when.

Like all of us, my uncertain voyage through the storm continues, because I am a mortal being in a fallen world. The day we saw that rainbow, just like the day we first saw Iguazu Falls, God wrote in big letters of His majesty.

He has been writing to me in a smaller font ever since.
Some days I can see that tiny print most clearly through my tears.

DAY 18

Mundane Matters

"Don't forget to check on me!"

As years have gone by, I wish I'd taken a photo of this once-common event.

Every night my four-year-old daughter would climb out of bed, open her bedroom door, and stick her piggy-tailed head into the evening hallway with this not-so-gentle reminder.

"Checking" was more than being tucked in for the night. We did that first. Hours later, she expected us to open her creaky door and let the hallway light and older sibling sound into her dark, quiet room. I refused, because it seemed it would wake her up rather than calm her down. So, I pretended to check on her. But she always knew the next morning. "You didn't check on me!" It was my husband who decided to comply. Every single night. And because of that routine, she knew she could count on her dad when something big came up.

UNDERSTANDING MUNDANE

While this good father was routine, I always believed that Father God is not. Most of my life I associated God mostly with raising people from the dead, multiplying loaves and fishes, and parting seas. I couldn't conceive of Him as mundane because He seemed unpredictable and so far from human-ordinary.

The definition of *mundane* seemed to support my belief: *monot-*

onous, unvarying, repetitive, routine, everyday, expected, conventional, earthly. Its antonyms include *extraordinary, imaginative, heavenly, spiritual.*

Much of life here on Earth is mundane, dull, and uneventful. Paul David Tripp, in his book *Age of Opportunity*, suggests there are not many grand moments in this life; we live in the utterly mundane: in the hallways, drive-throughs, and laundry rooms of life. But Tripp adds, there is good news: This is where our character is set and refined.

Most importantly, the ordinary is where we learn to trust our extraordinary God.

CONSISTENCY IS KEY

Like my daughter, I also had a kind, constant earthly father.

Growing up, traveling was a rare event for our farm family. Our first vacation was a trip to Pikes Peak when I was about nine or ten. I recall being shocked when we got to 14,110 feet and it was snowing that July. But honestly, I don't remember much else about that vacation. Even after all the planning and driving and squabbling in the backseat that surely took place, it just doesn't stand out in my memory. Honestly, without the pictures, I might have forgotten that we even went.

But I do remember in detail how Dad wrote with a sharpened yellow pencil on a white paper dinner napkin every morning, drinking sugar-laced coffee from a glazed ebony cup. Figuring and calculating his day, even if he had gone to sleep in the wee hours of the morning, weary from harvest. Sitting in the same chair when I came down the stairs to catch the bus from the time I was in first grade until I graduated from high school. And I vividly remember Mom making dinner from scratch every night and setting the table for the entire family, even when she had worked at another job all day. I remember the careful casseroles and loading the olive-green dishwasher with the Corelle salad bowls.

As if it were Ground Hog Day again and again and again until I got my part right.

I could count on Mom and Dad for their part, and I knew it.

Sometimes the fact that something is mundane is what makes it unusual. Like the steadiness of my parents in my childhood, and now my husband checking on our children and me. He does every bit of our once-shared housework since my chronic illness diagnosis. The very ordinariness of these acts makes them special because it means they're constant—which is its own kind of extraordinary.

Children thrive on consistency, on ordinary. Especially children of God. Faith develops best in the comfort of constant care.

God demonstrated constancy for His people while they were in Egypt. Then, the children of Israel relied on God's daily guidance and sustenance through their decades-long wilderness trek. In the time of Judges, believers persistently forgot God, yet He repeatedly delivered them. Abraham, Hannah, Noah, Ruth…all experienced God's consistency too.

ORDNINARY PREPARES US FOR EXTRAORDINARY

God has always lived and worked within the ordinary, sad, wonderful rhythm of human life. He is a Master at making the mundane into the miraculous.

A boy's ordinary sack lunch became a crowd's feast.

A common jug of water became essential wedding wine.

A monotonous seven-day march around a city caused walls (and empires) to fall.

Years of lackluster shepherding produced a man after God's own heart.

An unremarkable young girl became the mother of the miraculous Savior.

And the ongoing miracle is this: His care doesn't stop at the empty womb or even at the empty tomb. As Immanuel—*God with us*—He continues to share in our not-so-special moments—the ones that form the bulk of our lives.

His miraculous goes on behind our everyday scenes, weaving into the fiber of our faith. The mundane shapes faith and prepares us to trust the Source of the unexpected. In faith and in life, it takes a constant supply of ordinary to prepare us for the extraordinary. We must have a history with our God to recognize when His majesty overcomes our humanity.

Such unexpected majesty showed up when God's persistent pillar pierced the Israelites' dark journey, forging their faith as they approached the Promised Land. It happened again when the psalm-steeped shepherds followed a particularly bright star pointing to the Savior of the world.

God was also at work when I came down with ordinary appendicitis. I left the hospital knowing that my end-stage heart failure had made a temporary turnaround.

From my journal:

The day after my unexpected appendectomy prompted a new heart test, the nurse practitioner who had delivered the first bad news about my heart failure visited me. Revealing a huge, unbelievable improvement in my heart function, she high-fived me, and I said, "I have so many questions!" Tearing up, she said, "We do too. You had us pretty worried. I don't want to say we had given up on you, but after sixteen months, the window of time for you to improve was getting pretty narrow. I don't get to see miracles every day, but you're definitely one of them. I'm so glad I got to be a part of this."

It wouldn't have meant anything to my nurse practitioner unless she had been there for every heartbreaking test and consultation with no improvement. She had to be with us in the mundane, monotonous months for this remarkable event to matter at all.

And we needed every bit of those unchanging months to recognize that our faithful God had actually been checking on us all along that dark path, through our medical team, our church, and our family. Even through a stream of texts, calls, and video chats from that grown-up piggy-tailed girl.

RETHINKING MUNDANE

My daughter's relationship with her dad, like mine with the Father, was formed by countless ordinary moments, and only a few extraordinary ones. We have snapshots of the exciting times, but we have a faith built of the mundane ones.

Perhaps I originally had the definition of mundane too limited. And perhaps the biggest truth in our world is something mundane and yet spiritual: The God of the miraculous is the God of the ordinary. And perhaps He is most present in the everyday moments of our lives.

Just as certain as He will be on the rare snowy mountaintop, He is there in the dark hallways and the doubt-filled hospital rooms. He shows up in the monotonous manna and joins us here by way of an ordinary feeding trough. His humble, common beginning positioned Him to infiltrate and redeem every insignificant moment.

Our extraordinary God is there.

Consistently checking on us every night.

DAY 19

Mosquitoes, Martians, and a Trustworthy God

"You'll never survive without bug spray. They have giant mosquitoes," my sister advised, tossing me a can of insect repellant.

The first week of July following third grade, I reluctantly packed my small mod-flowered suitcase to join my older siblings for a week at the fabled site Camp Wentz. I had seen a few grainy black and white snapshots from my sister's Kodak Instamatic the previous summer, but entering the gate, I realized the photos didn't do it justice. The cabins were tiny stone castles and the entire grounds felt like a fairy-tale kingdom. My shy, already-homesick heart warmed a bit as Mom dropped us off in Ponca City, Oklahoma. I didn't know anyone else my age attending, but how could such an idyllic place hurt anyone?

After settling into my assigned castle-cabin, I was given the week's schedule. Right away I noticed a welcome movie in the outdoor pavilion—pure magic in 1974.

Sometime near sundown, we cabinmates walked together to attend the showing. I was excited to have this older-kid experience. But the movie did not match the charmed Wentz vibe I had conjured up—it was *Invaders from Mars*. Perhaps not the best choice to show young children on their first night at a mosquito-prone camp.

QUESTIONING AUTHORITIES

In the film, a young boy, David, notices a personality change after seeing an unusual red puncture along the hairline on the back of his father's neck. He slowly realizes that others in town have this peculiar marking. They are also behaving in a cold and hostile manner: neighbors, teachers, policemen. David ultimately discovers that humanoid Martians have implanted mind control crystals in the brains of these adult authority figures.

I remember watching my counselors closely that week, always checking the back of their necks for the telltale red dot. *Bug bite or Martian meddling? Are these adults trustworthy?*

Seemed a strange thing to have to do in the middle of a kingdom.

This was the first time I questioned if the people I trust actually deserved my devotion, if they were concerned for my ultimate good. Not tainted or controlled by something foreign or corrupt.

DEFINING TRUST

Thankfully, most of my life I have not been disappointed with those I've placed my trust in, those charged with protecting and guiding me. But as an adult child of God, I have often found myself questioning the King Himself. Whether He is always good, always for me, always protecting me.

Can I trust Him?

According to Charles Pope, trust is the "stable conviction that whatever God decides to do is the right thing. It means being at peace with what He does, what He decides."

Trust is a belief in the *rightness* of what God says and does because of His nature.

It's not an assurance that everything will go our way or that God will offer an explanation when it doesn't.

But that He is solid and constant. That we can lean on Him as He holds our best interests close to His heart.

I had KP duty the second day of camp…on messy spaghetti night… with the mean eighth-grade boy. And I never understood why the only friend I was able to make wasn't allowed to join my afternoon activity group. The counselor felt a little cold and hostile, almost humanoid, to me. (I did a quick neck-check.) But those camp adults were consistent in safety and care. Just as we eventually learn about our parents, fallible as they are, I should have trusted them earlier.

Still, with chronic illness, trust is an expensive commodity, and I've had trouble trusting even my infallible God.

CAN GOD BE TRUSTED?

In the middle of my first downturn, I wrote this in my journal:

Got results of yesterday's echo. To our sad surprise, my heart function significantly decreased. We are a little numb from this sucker punch. We feel helpless in times like this, doing everything we can, and yet sometimes it slips from our hands. By now I know I should trust that God is totally in control. It is a difficult ask, with the doctors puzzled yet again. But even in the middle of this, I continue to be astounded by palpable grace. And I know my peace comes from a place outside myself, from this place of grace.

I'm developing a deep, though sometimes elusive, knowing that God's truth and strength remain unchanging. In spite of my health, which obviously isn't. Suffering will come whether we trust this God or not. Discounting God will not decrease our pain. It will just remove our source of grace. The difference is this: Trust brings grace and grace delivers peace. And that is what we all need more than anything.

If anyone ever wondered if God could be trusted, it was surely Paul. Under pressure far beyond what he could endure alone, Paul "despaired even of life itself" (1 Cor. 1:8) at one point. Blinded, shipwrecked, imprisoned, and eventually killed, Paul must have wondered if his God had turned cold and hostile. Through it all, Paul's messages leaned heavily on these two words, *grace* and *peace*. They solidify our understanding of a trustworthy God.

Peace to endure this life; grace to ensure the next.

My week at camp didn't turn out exactly like I'd dreamed. My life hasn't either. Not because those watching out for me weren't reliable, but because this broken world beckons us to desire something more, and I suspect it has something to do with Paul's grace and peace.

Somehow, I expected an easy life, and prayers answered in my way, in my time. I never expected grace and peace, which, turns out, is all I ever really needed.

MORE ACCURATE EXPECTATIONS

So, perhaps we need to unlearn some things.

Although God is always good and trustworthy, He never said our lives would be. In fact, He said just the opposite. God actually proved His trustworthiness by telling us in Ecclesiastes that this world would hurt. But the same God who told us our life would be hard also sent His Spirit to instill it with grace and peace.

This trustworthy God never gave up on rescuing us from an untrustworthy world. And even while we live out our short lives here, God never allows the Enemy to win. He constantly seeks our good within His perfect will.

"And we know that in all things God works for the good of those who love him, who have been called according to his purpose" (Romans 8:28 NIV).

Although we may not understand it or see it, we can rely on this truth from Paul's pen. Our trustworthy God said it, and even in the disappointing downturns, I have experienced the grace and peace to believe it.

Because even with so much uncertainty in my life, I already know the end of the story. Where castles and kingdoms are not miniature or manmade, where mind control crystals are exchanged for even riskier free will.

And, as in the entire plot, our King can always be trusted.

DAY 20

Both Sides of Water

After we extensively remodeled a house, we needed rain for our un-irrigated grass seed to sprout in the sweltering summer heat. In our amateur construction plans, the exterior door into the new mudroom was installed slightly below ground level. So, every time we got a hard rain that summer, the grass grew but the mudroom flooded.

And every time my husband and I would be in there barefooted (usually around 3:00 a.m.), desperately and unsuccessfully, pushing water back out the door with brooms. In the aftermath, we lost school projects, a dog dish, baseball cleats, and a bit of our sanity.

It seems the water we need to survive sometimes threatens to destroy us.

Growing up in a farm family, I learned this lesson early on. The same rains that we prayed to fall so we could grow the crop, we prayed to end so we could harvest it. And ultimately, we surrendered to the precipitation that seemed to control the entirety of our lives.

GOOD AND BAD TOGETHER

Water, like my life, has often appeared to have two opposing sides: good and bad.

My introspective son frequently surprised me with quips far beyond his years. At eight years old, he confidently told me, "There's a little bit of good and a little bit of bad in everything." How could that little boy know that life's good and bad always flow in the same stream? He must have realized that the water we were fighting in the mudroom had some good in it.

Author God uses this dichotomous idea extensively. Water metaphors appear hundreds of times throughout the Bible. And they all take on one of two themes: trouble or salvation. Water represents the good and the bad in life. It ruins and it restores; it contaminates and it cleanses.

"Save me, O God, for the waters have come up to my neck" (Psalm 69:1 NIV).

"With joy you will draw water from the wells of salvation" (Isaiah 12:3 NIV).

Through my illness, I have discovered that rather than representing individual contradictory ideas, these water images actually reflect a process: setback to salvation. Water bookends any spiritual journey. It represents trouble we can't humanly control so we can be washed in His saving current.

Water's two sides are the full picture of God's plan to bring us close to Him.

He knew we'd have to feel the rising water to need a rescue.

He knew grace would mean nothing if we aren't saved from anything.

He knew we'd have to experience hopelessness to appreciate holiness.

RAINS FOR A REASON

Still, most of us would rather avoid the treacherous side of water and skip right to the saving stream. But our God never allows spiritual shortcuts.

Many times in God's continuing story, trials that were not averted, floods that still came rushing in, drew the sufferer nearer to the heart of God: Paul in prison, Daniel in the den, Joseph in slavery, Jesus in Gethsemane.

And even me, in the rising waters of heart failure.

"Indeed, we felt that we had received the sentence of death. But that was to make us rely not on ourselves but on God who raises the dead" (2 Cor.1:9 ESV).

God wants us to know firsthand that He is far greater than anything we will face, far greater than our pain. So He allows uncomfortable, even bruising parts of life to happen. As Rick Warren says, "God is more interested in our character than in our comfort." God wants more than anything to develop in us a character that will see us through eternity. Into everlasting with Him.

And our good God knew that such intimacy would require both sides of water.

So, I am learning to appreciate the difficult side of water. Charles Spurgeon put it this way, "I have learned to kiss the waves that throw me up against the Rock of Ages."

BECOMING CLOSER

Near the end of the remodel, we were up to our necks in stress. My husband and I were uncharacteristically at odds with one another. Family members had tragically died far too young. Construction costs were blowing past even the highest estimates. Life was spinning out of control. Yet somehow, I got tickled during another early morning mudroom flood. Maybe from exhaustion, maybe from the sheer ridiculousness of the task. Maybe from the sight of my husband in his underwear and flip-flops, holding a push broom. It was the kind of tickle that cramps your stomach to try to contain. Before long, we were both laughing. I suddenly remembered how much I loved that carefree high school boy turned devoted dad. And I knew, in spite of everything we were facing, I'd choose him all over again.

But I might not have seen it if it hadn't been for the flood.

On our way back from a disappointing checkup on my heart failure, I made this journal entry:

The trip was both good and bad. Always good to spend uninterrupt ed time with my best friend. The first part of the trip was carefree, as we were unsuspecting of the bad news we were about to receive. We are driving through hard rain in Indiana now. We have no umbrella. And it occurs to me that storms often catch us off guard. So, it is probably no coincidence that gallons of water are pouring onto the pavement as we drive. The health storm is here again. But this time, I am less afraid. I'm remembering we have an ark. We just have to choose to climb aboard. Again.

Good and bad continue in intermingling streams. And my God and I have become closer because of it all. Just like my husband and I did in that mudroom.

The mudroom should have been a weak link in our relationship, a bad memory. But the mudroom, my illness, your detour, are the points where we consider our options. To give up on this God or choose the relationship again. To climb aboard the Ark or face the flood alone.

Through life's storms, I have gained a better understanding of who He is. Not a God who gives me everything I want, but a God who will part the seas to bring me closer to Him.

After all, the rainbow doesn't promise it will never rain again.

It promises when it does rain, even when it seems all of life is flooding, He has it under control. This God who works in both sides of water.

DAY 21

A Lapse of Faith

"You, too!"

The fate of my every day hung on those two words.

Before I climbed aboard the school bus heading for fourth grade, I made a ritual of saying to my mother, "Have a good day." Sometimes she would hear me and respond, other times she would be distracted by three other school-aged children and ignore me or just nod. I would then slowly repeat, "Have…a…gooood…daaay," piercing her with raised eyebrows, attempting to draw out the requisite response. (I was not above pretending to forget a book or mitten so I could run back into the house and have another stab at it.)

LOOKING FOR REASSURANCE

I needed to hear that she was on my side as I traipsed the scary outside world. To solidify what I already held in my heart.

I needed outward proof to sustain the inward knowing.

Many times in my life I've needed such assurances from God to bridge faith lapses. And Scripture suggests I'm not alone.

I remember identifying early on with shaky Gideon laying out the fleece during a lapse like mine. But as an adult with a chronic, progressive disease, I think more often about John the Baptist sitting in prison, facing almost certain death. We both experienced a lapse despite a deep faith in this God.

We both yearned for a clear message: "Are You the Expected One (the Messiah), or should we look for someone else?" (Matthew 11:3 AMP).

Because, what I'm living is not like anything I expected.

Like John, I know that if I've got this all wrong, now would be a good time to find out. But how could John not know? How could I not know? We both had witnessed His glory and His Spirit.

Still, weary from physical and spiritual skirmishes and foggy expectations, and with so much on the line, we needed reassurance. One more time.

God, You're usually tuned in. But You're not acting like Yourself lately. Is this my lapse or yours?

DEFINING *LAPSE*

A lapse of faith is different from full-blown abandonment. In the early church, *lapsi* referred to those who publicly renounced their faith under persecution, only to return to it in safer times. *Lapse* is a temporary decline or deviation from an expected state, slipping from a standard when the going gets tough.

It happened to me as I faced a health crisis in my life that I couldn't reconcile with what I knew to be true about my God.

A lapse is a faith soft spot, a weak fitting. It's when life draws us onto an unexpected path and we continue in faith, with caution tape around the question. *I'm doing this, Lord, but I need some scaffolding. I feel like I'm falling. I need to know You are real.*

After a sudden, unexpected (and I felt undeserved) diagnosis of end-stage heart failure, and years managing its ups-and-downs, I have felt the expanse of the lapse: A year and a half with no improvement despite round-the-clock prayer chains and the best medical team available. Then unexpected restoration, followed by unexplained declines.

I have confided in my husband that I don't even necessarily want to be fully healed. That would be fine, of course, but what I really wanted was just to see God working, even just a little. To know He is there, and listening, and knowing.

Like John, I needed words from God to span the faith divide.

WORDS MATTER

In fourth grade when my mother would answer, "You, too," I knew they were just words. And yet, naïve as I was, I knew that words matter. Even just two of them.

We all know the power of a pair of simple words:

"Thank you."

"I'm sorry."

"I do."

"Heart failure."

"I AM."

Just two tiny words can make all the difference. When nothing we're living changes, but the lapse is bridged.

Rather than deliverance from the condition, God often uses words to span the expanse between Him and His child. He uses His Word: "In the beginning was the Word, and the Word was with God, and the Word was God.…The Word became flesh and made his dwelling among us" (John 1:1,14a NIV).

True to His nature, in two-word segments, Jesus sent the reassurance John the Baptist needed.

Go back
tell John
blind see,
lame walk,
lepers cleansed,
deaf hear,
dead raised,
gospel proclaimed.

Jesus sent this lifeline of familiar prophecy from Isaiah, knowing it would surely be recognized by John. A solid faith never mattered more than then.

THE SACRED GAP

Chronic illness has taught me that lapses can cause our faith to be suspended in time. And yet in that space, God actually buttresses our belief into something stronger than it would have been otherwise, able to face whatever the next may be. We need a bridge from our old expectations to our current reality. God recognizes this and is doing sacred work there.

From my journal after my first major post-recovery decline:

Driving for the first time since being back from the Cleveland Clinic, my errand-occupied mind cleared briefly enough to recognize a familiar feeling—space between me and God. The empty expanse where I can't reach Him, or maybe He can't reach me. With my heart function down to where it was two years ago, all my interim progress is gone. He didn't finish the story the way I wanted Him to. Inside my car, I rolled up to a stoplight and yelled at God: Why not? What now? Then, all cried out, I turned on the radio and heard the lyrics, "Even if You don't, my hope is You alone." And I knew He heard me.

The most beautiful part of a faith lapse is that God always sends an answer to bridge it. The answer is not always a yes, not always on our time, not always relief from our circumstances. But it always brings the peace we need to span the emptiness. His grace is sufficient to carry us through the lapse. And that grace and peace will be two of this life's sweetest gifts.

As in the case of John the Baptist, my situation has not been reversed, but my faith has been reinforced. Reassurance has been delivered by fellow believers who have dared cross into my prison of pain and uncertainty.

I'm here.

Jesus saves.

God loves.

Prayer works.

Just as my mother's response did all those years ago, God's outward assurance fortified my faith. Nothing profound. Just simple, precious words to carry me through the emptiness.

So on those lapse days, despite my determined faith, I find myself asking if He is the One, if all this has meaning, if He is looking out for singular me in a sea of humanity. And if I listen closely, I often hear Him answer through the lips of others, with the two words I need to hear.

You, too.

DAY 22

Recency Syndrome

My oldest child was enamored with her dad from the very beginning. They had a relationship I wasn't sure I'd ever permeate. Everyone knew about their special bond.

When she was just learning to talk and interact, our family friend played a game with her. His good-natured teasing was designed to challenge that relationship. Across restaurant tables, he would ask my bright-eyed toddler which she loved more, candy or rocks. She would repeat, "rocks." Then, "Which do you love more, goldfish or rocks?" "Rocks." "Puppies or rocks?" "Rocks." Then, knowing she was warmed up, "Which do you love more, Daddy or rocks?" "Rocks." We would all laugh and my husband would grimace. But my daughter had no idea what she had done.

Often without even realizing it, we believe whatever we hear, see, or experience last.

A DANGEROUS BIAS

It's called recency syndrome, the tendency to remember more easily those events that have recently occurred. When I taught Supervision for college business majors, we covered this topic in terms of employee performance reviews. It can be a dangerous bias in business, but even more threatening in our spiritual lives.

Not long ago, I strolled into the Cleveland Clinic expecting a routine heart checkup. After over two years at the low end of normal, keeping chronic heart failure in check, I was first broadsided with the news that my heart function had significantly decreased.

At that point, my last notable encounter with God seems not so favorable. Recency syndrome might dictate that He is not a good Father. My latest recollection is not of His care.

Daddy or rocks?

Rocks.

Words showed up on my chart that we all thought had long been erased: "Left ventricle severely dilated." Again.

The doctors scrambled. "Maybe an ablation could help."

My first thought: *too little, too late.*

But ultimately, it is too soon. Too soon to judge God's course or character or care.

There is a difference in the following two statements, although factually, they are identical: *I'm alive, but I'm not healed.* And, *I'm not healed, but I'm alive.* The last phrase on our lips is the emphasis. And it is what we believe most in our hearts unless we remind our heads that ours is a more enduring God.

CRISIS TO CROWN

Joseph believed in a God of the long-term. He resisted the pull of the recency syndrome. He chose knowing that the pit and the slavery did not tell the full story of his life or his God. Even when the recent feels like evil, or confusion, or suffering.

"[Y]ou meant evil against me, but *God meant it for good*" (Genesis 50:20a ESV, emphasis added).

Joseph's short-term twelve-year crisis ultimately provided a crown so he could save his family.

Who knows what God has in store for us from the unexpected path? As Max Lucado explains, "In God's hands intended evil becomes eventual good."

Rocks become gifts. A crisis becomes a crown. And the secret sauce is time.

When I had to discipline my children, I sometimes worried that something would happen to them (or to me) and the last conversation we had, their last memory or mine, would be that conflict. But our family had a history, a life we had formed together. It was silly of me to worry that all they would know of me would be our last interaction. And yet, too often we do that with God.

This cheapens God's love for us by reducing it, and Him, to a linear timeline.

To only remembering rocks.

And it is unfair to judge God's character and love for us by how long it's been since He answered a prayer the way we'd like.

One snapshot, or even a curated collection, cannot capture the essence of our amazing God. His dynamic nature could never be reduced to that. Joseph, disowned by his brothers, refused to let a single event sway his faith or paint the full portrait of his God.

Now as I face the future, perhaps healed as I will ever be, recency syndrome threatens to dictate the nature of my God. As Christians in a fallen world, we all fight it daily. We can choose the last experience as total truth, or we can believe in the God of the long-term. We can remember a God who recently disappointed us or remember the God of our entire lives.

For Christians, the "No" is only the short-term version of the full-length story, the one seen through the foggy, near-sighted lens of this world. As Frederick Buechner says, "The Gospel is bad news before it is good news."

GOD OF THE LONG-TERM

So our lives often go.

Sometimes in a faithful life, circumstances get worse, not better. Faith in God's future grace for us, in His long-term plan, is what sustains us in those desperate moments.

As I look back at my journal, some days I have been distressed and doubtful. But in the full-version account, I can now see He is faithful.

And the Journal of the Ages, the Bible, reminds us all of God's longsuffering love and care.

One year into my diagnosis, I wrote this journal entry, waiting to see what God would do:

He may heal me and He may not. He is always about something deeper: making our lives eternally significant. Sometimes that takes getting our attention with a healing or an answer to a physical prayer, but not always. He is always in the business of saving our soul, at whatever cost to Him, or to us.

Like Jesus' story, Joseph's story is the saga of the entire Bible. And of each of our lives. A story of a crisis first, and then a crown. And trusting in the long-term God who walks with us through it all.

He has always stressed the enduring over the immediate, personal knowing instead of facts, deep relationship rather than duties. And only through His eternal Spirit do we become something bigger, sturdier, longer-lasting than we are.

Crisis or crown?

Daddy or rocks?

The challenge is to remember the entire story, not just the part we're living. Maybe it takes all the chapters, not just the most recent ones, for the story to make sense.

Maybe it takes both Daddy and the rocks.

Just as it takes both the crisis and the crown.

DAY 23

Locust Years

Locusts don't invade wheat farms in southcentral Kansas.

At least they didn't when I was growing up there. But plenty of other pests did.

And grasshoppers sure could make a mess of a family garden overnight. Now as a resident of wooded northwest Arkansas, I've learned a placid deer family can decimate a suburban yard of prized hostas in short order.

Mom used her fair share of Co-op chemicals to fight the garden battle. Even with deer-off spray, nets, and a fast 'n fierce wiener dog, my husband and I can't seem to win.

All those years ago, grasshoppers ate into our canning reserves for the year: pickles and okra, corn and green beans. Now deer eat into our landscape aesthetic and wreck it until the next spring. In both cases, we've been powerless to restore our labor-infused plantings.

REDEEMING THE PAST

In the Old Testament, God promises the people of Israel He will make things right again, despite the disaster of a four-year locust invasion.

"I will restore to you the years that the swarming locust has eaten" (Joel 2:25 ESV).

A perplexing promise in the middle of crushing uncertainty.

From my journal:

Not long ago, I had heart failure with restored EF, but now I'm back down to heart failure with reduced EF. Despite my survival, I can't help but feel that these years have been wasted somehow. Years of diligence for nothing...titrating meds, eliminating sodium, dealing with constant fatigue, rearranging my life. All futile water under the bridge. What lies ahead now? And would this be a different story if I had acknowledged the symptoms years ago?

Years the locusts have eaten.

Like annual crops and hosta, years that have been eaten are gone for good.

Time passes and never returns.

We've all felt that disappointed pang when we glance in the rearview mirror. For most of us, that mirror is splattered with locusts and the irreparable damage they have caused. We see reflections of years we could have lived differently or better.

Locust years are years that beg for a mulligan, a do-over, a second run at it. I often lament about being on a path I didn't choose. But sometimes because of missed opportunities or poor choices, we find ourselves on a path we *did* choose and we carry heavy regret.

God knows this, and He has made a way to make it new again. Whether our past locust years number in the single digits or in the sixties, whether by misguided choice or by unchosen circumstance, God promises to redeem them all.

RECLAIMING THE FUTURE

But He promises even more.

Locust years are also future years that have been taken from us because of what has happened. Maybe we lost a loved one far too soon, a crumbled marriage deprived us of a lifelong companion, a failed career or business venture robbed us of a secure retirement. Or, maybe like me, the illness locusts have swarmed in.

Losses can affect far more than our past. Because of what we have lost, our future is threatened too.

On my childhood farm, Dad would save some of his best wheat crop as seed for the following planting season. If hail or drought or even too much rain ruined a year's harvest, it also affected the seed that would grow future ones. A bad year could reach far into the future.

Locust invasions in the Bible had a similar multi-year impact. For the Israelites, the harvest was wiped out for four straight years. Grape vines and fruit trees took years to re-establish and bear fruit again. As in my childhood, the grain harvest lost for the current year robbed seeds from the next.

Our devastation can span many years as well. We need God to restore not only our past but also our future. The problem is our current loss often blinds us.

Writer Scott Hubbard says, "Our worst days have a way of burying the mercies of God in our past and darkening the promises of God for our future."

What has happened can create regret for the past and also destroy our hope for the future.

But Jehovah is a God of wonders. He promises what seems impossible.

He is promising to fill the bare stalks of remorse in our souls.

He is promising to make our foggy future bright with hope.

He is promising restoration.

AS IF IT NEVER HAPPENED

Restore is to bring back, reinstate, make good as new. As if it never happened…

As if the locusts had never invaded.

As if heart failure, or cancer, or MS had never been the diagnosis.

As if the opportunity had never been squandered.

As if the relationship had never ended.

That's how our God's grace-filled heart works. Not just compensated for, not just making it up to us in some sort of counter-balancing way. But restoration, as if it never happened.

Our God is unbound by time. He can completely redeem both our past and our future. God works everything together to restore what sin and a broken world have cost us. Whatever the locusts have done to destroy our testimony or the life of a prodigal we know, He is ready to restore it all. On both sides of time.

It is His nature and it is His heart. And above all, it is His promise.

Charles Spurgeon says of locust years, "This promise is only fulfilled by the exceeding grace of God." If we can release our grip on the pen, not only will God write our story, but His grace will right it too.

Standing in a locust-stripped field, or a grasshopper-invaded garden, or even just a deer-decimated yard, restoration can seem a long way off. But God sees us. He knows our story. Right now, heaven and earth are being moved by a faithful God who has already determined the outcome of our situations. And He's got a long list of references from His restoration business:

- Moses, murderer chosen by God to lead the Israelites out of slavery
- David, adulterer who became a man after God's own heart
- Rahab, prostitute whose bloodline produced the Son of God
- Paul, Christian-killer who authored most of the New Testament
- Zacchaeus, despised tax collector who left a faithful legacy for his family

Forgiveness, grace, and the resurrection itself are based on restoration. In fact, the entire Bible is the story of God restoring man's relationship to Him. Of making both our past and future good as new again. As if the disaster never happened.

Seems we can trust that He's got these locust years.

Meanwhile, I'll keep rewarding my little dachshund for chasing Bambi's extended family out of my front yard.

DAY 24

Languishing & Loaned Words

It was a subject of every parent-teacher conference that year, and it lived on into my adulthood. It still has legs, even today.

It was significant enough and memorable enough that Dad and I reminisced about it during his last weeks, and he even included it in the written account of his life that we are all so grateful he took time to document.

It was the puzzling period in middle school I've never been able to explain. The months I kept forgetting my math book.

I had homework each night and needed that book. I knew it. But somehow, I fritzed out every afternoon just before dismissal. I remember opening the hinged top of my desk and resting it on my hunched head. I was attempting to establish a safe place to concentrate long enough to remember, quickly enough to not miss the bus. Still, two or three times a week for months on end, that math book didn't make it home with me.

My dad was friends with the principal so after my tearful outburst, Mom would make a long-distance call to my dad's office. Long after they both should have been home, Dad would convince the principal to meet him back at the school to get my book. Somehow, I was okay with Mom asking Dad, and Dad asking the principal. I was happy to have them speak for me.

I'm sure there is discussion to be had about that method of parenting and the value of natural consequences, but that is for another day.

As I look back on it, I can now see that something bigger was going on. This painful scenario kept happening and I felt powerless to prevent it. And for some reason, totally against my organized, can-do personality, I shrunk back.

I knew I was stuck.

I didn't know I was languishing.

LANGUISHING IS NOT NEW

To *languish* means to become spiritless or weak, but at the same time dazed and confused. It happens when you're trapped somewhere in a tight place or an uncomfortable circumstance.

A prisoner might languish in jail, longing for freedom.

A patient might languish in illness, desiring relief.

A person might languish in sin, waiting for redemption.

Everything is at once too overwhelming and not engaging enough. Each task requires a Herculean stretch of motivation. We are tired, burned out, and unexcited but also restless, eager to engage, and trying.

In Psalm 6:2, David felt it. "Be gracious to me, O Lord, for I am languishing; heal me, O Lord, for my bones are troubled" (ESV).

Since my own ongoing health issues, psalms like this have become a friend to me, an advocate. And I'm starting to understand why.

"The Psalms have a unique place in the Bible because [while] most of Scripture speaks to us, the Psalms speak for us." —Athanasius of Alexandria

A DIFFICULT DÉJÀ VU

The heaviness of languishing intensifies when it keeps happening. Like my repeated math book debacle.

I realize now that as we waited for the office to call the bus students, my teacher had started a routine of "math races" where students went to the board two at a time, were given a long division problem, and worked them at high speed in front of the class. The winner was given so much classroom acclaim. I felt like I was on the daily display of my life. The constancy of the competition was just too much for introverted me.

When we languish like this, we get caught in the crummy cadence and we lose our way. We feel stuck, in sort of a cyclical limbo where life buzzes around us, but we can't seem to join in.

It's where we all are as depression resurges or an illness resurfaces or the struggle reemerges. It's a difficult déjà vu, a repeated rewind.

How am I here after I thought I was so far past it?

How am I still struggling when I was sure it would be over by now?

Any stressful, ongoing condition can cause us to languish. Grief is a type of languishing. We languish when we continually carry heavy financial burdens or harbor family worry for decades. Chronic illness can cause it too.

From my journal:

It's finally starting to sink in that this condition really is "chronic." It's constant. I keep wondering, "How is this still mine to do?" If I'm lucky, my heart function will remain where it is, at this low level. Several years ago, I thought I was overcoming heart failure, then a couple years later my heart function dropped 40 percent. At my last appointment, doctors started discussing whether the original "near-normal" reading was even accurate. It's an all too familiar "here we go again" heartache. I feel numb.

Again, David's words seem loaned just to me as I languished. "How long, Lord? Will you forget me forever? How long will you hide your face from me?" (Psalm 13:1 NIV).

LOOKING UP

It seems common consensus that the way out of the stranglehold of languishing is with something called *flourishing.*

Psychologists tout it now, and David mentioned it too. In Psalm 52, on the run from King Saul, in the middle of all kinds of deep trouble, David was able to say, "But I am like an olive tree flourishing in the house of God; I trust in God's unfailing love for ever and ever" (vs. 8

NIV). David wasn't in denial. He knew his situation. But he chose to concentrate instead on what he knew about his God.

David knew this: "When we can't trace God's hand, we must trust His heart." —Charles Spurgeon

Flourishing only happens with a renewed focus, concentrating on something outside yourself. David chose to focus on God's heart, the only constant he knew.

In the thick of peril, the man who all his flawed life chased after God's heart, David wrote Psalm 121. "I lift my eyes to the hills. From where does my help come? My help comes from the LORD who made heaven and earth" (Psalm 121: 1–2 ESV).

Fix your eyes on the only One who can deliver you from the paralyzing hopelessness you're feeling. Focus. Don't look anywhere else. Just look up.

Often we can't change the circumstances that cause us to languish. And for reasons we may never understand, God chooses not to.

But those periods of languishing were part of making David who God intended him to be. And they're making us into who we are meant to be as well. Like David, we should focus less on waiting for our world to change, and more on how our hearts can change for the better. The simple, difficult way is by looking up in the middle of it all, to Him.

WHEN WE HAVE NO WORDS

If only I'd taken my head out of my desk and looked up, I would have found my help too. Somehow in my languishing, I had never been able to make a list, to simply write down my homework for the day. But my good teacher summarized our daily assignments on the upper corner of the board for us. It was never up to me to remember that book on my own.

Those stressful math races continued all year, getting even more complex and competitive. But once I saw that reminder, once I took the focus off the trouble at hand, I found a way through. And more importantly, I found the written words of a trusted person to lean on.

I've been grateful all my life for words that spoke for me when I couldn't, including cards and texts from faraway friends. Written prayers I found of my mother's that she prayed daily over me in my early diagnosis when I couldn't. And the repeated words of my dad to my principal, asking for my book. Then later in both our lives, weekly encouragement calls.

Now, the Psalms do that speaking for me in difficult times.

Thanks to my parents' unadvised approach to parenting, I started learning some life lessons that year in middle school. How getting stuck happens in this stressful life. How we need to look up to live through it.

And how the borrowed words of others can make all the difference between languishing and flourishing.

DAY 25

In the Shadow of a Stump

Some Scriptures seem to overpromise.

Like the one about how believers can run and not grow weary, how we can soar on wings like eagles (Isaiah 40:31). I can't remember ever running (or believing for something long-term) without getting super exhausted. And heart failure makes it nearly impossible to soar.

My husband, on the other hand, is a marathon runner. He's good. He ran the NYC marathon and the Boston. So, you get the picture when I tell you he runs. He's logged thousands of miles, shed oceans of sweat, and worn out dozens of shoes. During those runs, my husband prays for the schools, people we know as he runs past their houses, government offices, businesses, churches. And he takes mental note along the way.

He ran past a stump and he took me back to it later in the day.

It is a dramatic stump. In fact, you barely notice the historic house on the same lot. Sitting in the middle of a front yard, a hope-filled tree must have one day been planted with dreams of a shaded picnic, maybe a bird house, or even a tire swing or treehouse. But that tree and all the idyllic plans clearly died, and the stump has been carved into a prominent pole-like structure topped with an ornate bald eagle.

When I first saw the house, I thought, Good for them. They are embracing that stump. (And it's an impressive one). They are making the best of a bad situation.

That was a couple years ago.

Deep into my diagnosis, I am weary from a recurring battle I somehow never expected, fighting to not be defined by this disease. Struggling to make my life about more than the weak heart inside my body.

I now question that ornate stump. I wonder why the homeowners would rather highlight the dead tree and miss the grand house behind it, and more importantly, the lives inside.

The imposing stump in front of that house represents the struggle I am feeling. And I have a hunch I'm not alone.

STUMPS CAN DEFINE US

Even before we have stumps to contend with, we ask it. We're all born with this persistent question inside us: *Who am I?* We struggle with resumes, applications, and even introductions well into adulthood. To answer this question, we turn to roles and relationships, positions and possessions.

And worse, sometimes what threatens to define us is not even something we love, but something we fight. Because our scars are real and raw, we can idolize our suffering, our role as a sufferer. We often place our worth in how we endure, instead of in Whose we are.

Sometimes, like that house my husband found, our identity can be overtaken by a stump called chronic illness or infidelity, bankruptcy or infertility, without even realizing it.

Who am I?

Am I defined by the stump?

Because all this has happened, will all of me be consumed in all of it?

Will my life story always be overshadowed by this circumstance?

ENGULFED BY A SHADOW

Priscilla Shirer says, "There's a difference between where you've been, what you've done, what has happened to you, and who you are."

Our good God defined the edges of our identity a long time ago. *I am more than this temporary detour. I am not this stump. I am an eter-*

nal child of God. Still, as much as we know about Whose we are, our life circumstance often overwhelms our faith.

We call that house my husband ran past "The Stump House" now. Onlookers can't even see the house anymore, because the stump steals the show. This was a stump that has been more than embraced, it has become the major moment of this front yard. The stump has cast a shadow and defined that address.

A shadow is created when something blocks the light. Scripture often uses the word *shadow* to indicate darkness, doom, and death. But any of life's dead ends can block His Light and cast a shadow over our identity. For me, it's been ongoing illness. From my journal:

Some days I feel my life becoming overshadowed by my disease. I want this challenge to change my life, but not be in charge of my life. I read today about a study that found heart disease can dictate a patient's identity. It's a phenomenon called "Illness Identity." In varying degrees, the disease has been found to infiltrate and sometimes overtake a person's identity. Worst case is engulfment, where the disease dominates your identity. Best case is enrichment, where the disease causes positive changes in your identity, with a couple of intermediate stages between. Not sure where I am, but I can see the real pull toward engulfment.

Whether from our own mistakes, ricocheted consequences of someone else's decision, or just living in a fallen world, we've all faced disappointment, stumps made from sawed-off hopes and withered plans.

And worse than eclipsing our identity in Christ, our stumps can sometimes obscure our view of Him.

Best remembered for bringing the Ten Commandments down from Mount Sinai, Moses had some failures and disappointments too. He had a few stumps that threatened to define his life and overshadow his God. Targeted at birth, raised outside his family, Moses then made some missteps of his own, killing the Egyptian for abusing his people. I'm sure as Moses was on the run for murder, his view of God seemed blocked.

But Moses's story wasn't over.

A different kind of shadow was on its way.

ANOTHER KIND OF SHADOW

The Spirit mentions another type of shadow throughout Scripture. And it speaks to protection and comfort.

"How priceless is your unfailing love, O God! People take refuge in the shadow of your wings." (Psalm 36:7 NIV).

Scripture and science agree: A shadow blocks the brightness of Light, but a shadow also blocks the heat of danger.

Here's one thing I've learned: We can struggle in the shadow of the stump, or we can shelter in the shadow of His wings. And maybe it takes both to fully experience God's provision.

Moses and the Israelites faced a stump or two while they wandered their desert for four decades. But they didn't walk around alone. They carried with them the Ark of the Covenant. For early believers, it was one of the most important symbols of God's presence. No coincidence it was topped by wings outspread. Despite dozens of disappointments, disasters, and dangers, Moses and his people found God's presence under protective wings.

We drove by the Stump House again yesterday. This time I saw outstretched wings on it that I hadn't noticed before, because I had focused so much on the sheer size of it. Maybe those wings were a reminder to me. *Though stumps may cast a shadow, so do His Wings.*

Let me tell you something about my husband, the marathon runner who found this interesting stump. He didn't start running until after we were married and had three children. His running was prompted by an emotional trauma. When he was thirty-eight, my husband lost his mother, his younger sister, and his father, all within two years. He had an opportunity for the losses to define him and his God. And to be honest, they did for a while. But now these heartbreaks are just a chapter, or several chapters, in his life. It is not the whole story or even the focus of it. Like Moses, my husband didn't let the stumps overshadow his life. He focused on the shadow of his Father's wings instead.

Ann Voskamp reminds us, "Whatever has happened doesn't define who you happen to be."

Or the One who happens to be taking care of you.

Scripture never promises we won't experience the worst the world has to offer. But it does promise that when we do, we won't be overtaken and we won't be alone. Like being tucked inside my father's jacket on the first unexpectedly cold fall day, sometimes the shadowy darkness is more about being taken care of in the middle of the unanticipated.

When taken in its entirety, much like our lives, Scripture makes sense.

This side of eternity, stumps will cast a shadow on who we are.

And while it's often darker than we'd like, we are being sheltered.

Under God's wings, in all of life's shadows, we can run toward an unknown future.

And yes, even us non-marathoners can soar without growing weary or afraid.

DAY 26

Finding Answers in Unanswered Prayers

I begged my dad to say yes. I flashed my brown eyes at him, daring him to resist.

My eight-year-old mind just knew I could prove my maturity by being admitted to the Headless Woman carnival sideshow.

I remember her well. The version that made her rounds at the Kansas State Fair decades ago sat comfortably in her chair, legs tapping in tall shiny white go-go boots, a ribbed turtleneck, and a cute striped mini skirt. Against the foggy, curtained background, her neck seemed to be capped with a complicated life-sustaining device, a tangle of wires and tubes whirring and beeping and lights flashing.

After Dad granted my request, she showed up in my nightmares for years. Even worse, after that fair escapade, I was sure she was sitting in my bedroom closet every night, swinging her crossed booted leg as soon as the lights switched off.

I wish Dad would have said no to my request. As a mature adult now, those same brown eyes can still wince with fear in a dark, lonely room.

And yet sometimes that grownup girl can't understand why Father God doesn't seem to be listening to her requests and granting every one.

The Bible gives many reasons why God may not fully consider our prayers, from impure motives (James 4:3) to doubt (James 1:6), from poorly tended relationships (1 Peter 3:7) to ignoring justice and the needs of the oppressed (Isaiah 58:7–9). But what about when my motive is unselfish, when my faith feels strong, when I have cultivated good relationships and sacrificed for the good of others? What about unanswered prayers then?

GOD JOINS WITH US

Sometimes silence or apparent indifference from God feels cruel, as if He is ignoring us. But anyone who has parented understands that the no is often more difficult and more loving than the yes. As Andrena Sawyer says, "God is just as merciful in the things He does not allow, as He is in the things He does."

Make no mistake, God longs for us to pray. Sometimes, His answers are big miraculous ones. But sometimes they aren't. Sometimes He doesn't take us out of our trouble, but instead joins us there, in the middle of the silence and unexpected answers. And we discover a lifelong truth: It's easier to be in hard places with God than in those same inevitable places without Him.

In my own hindsight evaluation, I know unanswered prayers during my heart failure journey have developed my character and dependence on Him. From my journal:

Over the last four years, I've uttered a few "Why mes?" And sometimes I ask about healing, "Why not?" or about the struggle, "Why now?" but more often I'm asking for Him to be close, wherever this thing ends up. I'm not expecting Him to suspend natural laws like He did in the fiery furnace or in the lion's den, but to walk with me like in John the Baptist's prison cell or in Gethsemane. He doesn't seem intent on making this trouble disappear. God's silence or flat-out denial has forged a deeper hope and a release of control. And a solid trust in a more permanent bond to Him. I suppose that's what I should have been asking for from the beginning.

Maybe prayer was meant to be more about encountering God, and less about petitioning Him. Because when we encounter God as a relationship-seeking Father, bigger things always happen.

Ann Voskamp says, "We may not always get our miracle, but we always get God. And that is the miracle that is more than enough."

As evidenced by my attendance at the carnival sideshow, my dad was a pushover when it came to his brown-eyed girl. Though most of the lyrics escaped both of us, this was our song because we could decipher one line, "You're my brown-eyed girl." I was three when it came out. Dad sang it to me every time it crackled through his Chevy truck radio while I stood next to him on the vinyl bench seat as he drove, my arm around his neck. Whatever happened, we were bound together. I knew he loved me, and that was more than enough to get us through the tough times.

A LONGER-TERM PERSPECTIVE

Dad said yes to several things he shouldn't have (including some too-close-to-dinner Milky Way bars, a used VW, and a pet raccoon.) All of us parents have. But our heavenly Father who sees the long term does not.

When Lazarus was dying, Jesus did not answer pleas for healing. Instead, He had resurrection on His mind. And Jesus Himself asked for the cup of suffering to pass from Him, but God had a different, more amazing plan coming for that storyline as well.

When our own prayers feel unanswered, it might be that God wants something different for us too. And when He does, it's always something better, for our good and for His glory. We are wrapped together in that dual, eternal purpose.

Only a later perspective can fuel our faith in such a far-reaching God.

As much as he loved his brown-eyed girl, my own dad's human eyes could only see so far. But our God has different eyes. And sometimes we get a glimpse of His vision when the infertility ends in heart-warming adoption, or the pink slip results in a stellar new career. Just as God knew to delay or deny when I wanted that relationship or application to work out. I am now so relieved they didn't.

I'm grateful for conversations I had with my dad in hospice and with my mother as a widow that I never would have had, never did have, in the smooth, easy chapters of our family story.

THE GOD WHO SEES

Still, too often we don't see the finished end of prayer. So we need to find answered prayers in the silence of nonanswers and in the disappointment of different answers.

And we can only see it differently because He does.

This dismissive-seeming God is the same God who sees, *El Roi.* Seeing each one of us right where we are, and seeing to the end of time. Carefully sifting through outcomes and weighing consequences, with ultimate good in mind.

I wanted Dad's last PET scan to come back clean. God had done it before, and I knew He could do it again. I wanted my last echocardiogram to show my heart functioning normally again. God had already astonished doctors once and I knew He could pull off an encore performance.

In both cases, He chose not to. Why, I don't know. But I'm holding onto hope that He sees the entire picture, and His plan will somehow be a better one than mine.

Prayers, especially the ones not resolved in my way or in my lifetime, are to me more conundrum than conviction. But I know God listens. And I know prayer matters. And when waiting on an answer seems excruciating, I want to remember it is better to be standing still with this farsighted God than moving at break-neck speed without Him.

One day we will thank Him face to face for every answered prayer.

But just maybe (and perhaps even more importantly), we will fall at His feet in gratefulness for the unanswered ones.

A Question of Control

Days 27–39

. . . . .

Jesus's Desert Dilemma

"Again, the devil took him to a very high mountain and showed him all the kingdoms of the world and their splendor. 'All this I will give you,' he said, 'if you will bow down and worship me'" (Matthew 4:8–9 NIV).

What We Hear

My life trajectory is up to me.

Life Question

Is God's plan enough?

DAY 27

A Better Memory

The almost-antique farm truck is a strange combination of burned metal and rust from years of weathering. I remember the fire that caught our neighbors by surprise one hectic week in a June far behind us. Deep into the rush and importance of harvest, the truck was crossing the recently cut stubble to reach the combines. The dry straw sparked from the truck's heat. Before cell phones and with the nearest fire department at least twenty minutes away, the field and the truck were a total loss.

For decades on my way home to visit my parents, I noticed the truck still sitting in the overgrown field in the same spot it had burned, as if frozen in time or preserved as a monument.

That was a bad year. Wheat prices were falling, crops were poor, a late freeze threatened the young sprouts, an early drought endangered the mature stalks. Family farmers scratched their heads at their budgets and bills and pressed forward anyway. Harvest came that dry summer, right on time.

Now I look at that truck and I remember the harvests of my childhood. The days stretching past midnight, the pulling together to beat a hailstorm or to fetch a machine part, the chance to be part of something bigger than the children we were. And I remember praying for rain every dinner most summers, believing it was our only financial salvation.

Remembering is a special gift. It lets us see life in hindsight, to get the best perspective on God's constant care. We remember to see how high God can take us. And to never forget how low we can sink without Him. But it's not easy for any of us.

HUMANS ARE FORGETTERS

God's children have short memories. We forget the prayers He's answered, and more importantly, the ones He didn't that turned out better than our requests.

Like miracle-witnessing Peter who denied Christ, or the Israelites wandering in the desert, as life takes its toll on us, we lose sight of who He is. We already know how the Big Story ends, but in the middle chapters, we keep forgetting.

All of Christianity is built on remembering. While fulfilled prophesies firm up our belief, recollections of God's personal interventions feed our faith. God knew as much as we needed to remember, how easily we would forget. Holy Spirit invoked *remember* more than 150 times throughout Scripture, five times more often than *believe* and twice as often as *trust*. He knew we'd need ways to recollect His care.

Early on in my heart failure journey, my husband encouraged me to keep a journal to remember the whirlwind we found ourselves in. Those ugly first days I hesitated. I didn't ever want to reread or relive what was playing out. I scrawled painful words on a hospital notepad, and then in a notebook a friend dropped by my ICU room. I considered it catharsis, an attempt to drain the ugly doubt and disdain for God from my heart. I expected to never open them again.

There is great value in remembering, perhaps more than we may realize. Especially during shaky times. Many of us can feel like we're drowning in uncertainty when racial discrimination surfaces, natural disasters destroy, or a school shooting recurs. *What can I do?* One solid commitment we can make is to remember. As the headline flips to the next disaster or controversy or season, we can simply refuse to forget.

The key to moving forward when so much is still unresolved is to commit to having a better memory.

A NEED TO REMEMBER IT ALL

Sometimes I still drive slowly past the farm where I grew up. A new, unfamiliar family lives there now, tending to Mom's crimson cannas and to my make-believe backyard world. On the way "home," I still see that burned truck. Tears sneak up on me, knowing that this opportunity has vanished from our family's future. Like most of their neighbors, my parents relinquished their land to be used for a huge windfarm. They sold their equipment and moved into a nearby town.

Turbines the size of jets now tower over barns and even over that charred farm truck, dwarfing their importance on the landscape. Still, Dad called the windfarm a godsend. The monthly check provided more income than the farm ever could. But it was a painful change. Even as an adult child who lives states away, I detested seeing the land snatched up and the farmers moving away, or plowing now-tiny plots fractured by intrusive windfarm access roads.

Our word *remembrance* is derived from the Greek word *hupomimnesko. Hupo-* means *to come alongside.* The second part, *-mimnesko,* means *to remind.* Compounded, these words beckon us to come together and remind each other of the past. Some of what we should remember together is good: family celebrations, God's provision, healings, peace. But some of what we need to recall is painful: death, periods of need, illness, strife. It all shapes us and draws us into a deeper understanding of God's world and our place in it.

Looking back on the early pages of my journal has helped me remember how bad it really was and how far we have come.

For a "healthy" adult who's never been hospitalized (outside of childbirth), nurse tears feel unnatural. Also unnerving—doctors choking on their words and walking away mid-sentence to keep their composure. We feel like we're in the twilight zone. Jesus, walk here with us.

Despite so much hanging in the balance and so many prayers unanswered, it is necessary to remember the bad. Even Jesus asked us to remember the painful events of His death, over and over until He comes again. Remembering the hard will one day allow us to recognize God's provision. Recalling negative times also spurs us to become better than our younger selves, as a person and as a community.

NEVER AGAIN

I live a protected life, and like all mothers, I tried to protect my children. When we considered visiting the Holocaust Museum, I hesitated. I didn't want them to see evidence of the worst of their world. But in order to never repeat it, they had to look at it.

In order to honor history and the Holocaust slogan, "Never Again," we must remember.

"To forget a holocaust is to kill twice," wrote Noble laureate and survivor Elie Wiesel. Following a similar thread, Dr. Anthony L. Brown of University of Texas Austin, says of racial injustice after discovering his students didn't know about Rodney King, "One of the most effective ways to mold public perception is to allow the past to fade from the consciousness of future generations."

Erasing past pain makes all of today's striving worthless. And it is one of the most effective ways to lose your faith too.

We must remember the hard parts of our lives and our world. They make us wiser, better, closer.

Someday those mammoth wind turbines may sit rusted and motionless in a field as well. Some could see that as a failed experiment, as a sorrowful time when the family farm as we knew it disappeared from the southern Kansas landscape. But like the old truck in a burned-out wheat field, like the Holocaust Museum, like the racial injustice videos, like my old journal entries, we need to look at them. One day they will all be a reminder of how God provides a way when the way seems impossible to see. By recalling past pain, we continue to learn in this flawed world, and we are motivated to becoming more like Jesus.

He has promised to make all things new and just again one day.

He has so much invested in our future.

But for now, He's counting on us to do some difficult remembering.

DAY 28

Getting Okay with Giving Up

Following graduate school, my husband and I had a dream. We wanted to open our own accounting practice together, raise children in a small town, and grow old in a tight-knit community, closer to extended family. So, we started praying, hard. We applied for positions in smaller firms to get our foot in the door, to establish ourselves before putting out our own shingle. We had all the right motives. And we were near the top of our graduating class at a large university. We got several offers from the Big Eight national firms, but we got fewer bites from the smaller ones.

Finally, we secured an offer from a local office, just under market value. It was still a bit low, but in the area we wanted to live and someday build our practice.

We breathed a sigh of relief until the interviewer said, "That's for the both of you," indicating he was pricing us as a set. I remember looking at my young husband and wincing. Just like that, our expected salaries had fallen in half. Needless to say, we weren't okay with that.

After months of praying, we weren't sure what to do. The clock was ticking on accepting a job. *Should we keep praying? Should we pray even harder?*

I've always embraced the pit-bull-approach to prayer. Get ahold of it and never release until you get the result you want. Because God honors desperate, determined petitions, like Hannah's for her long-awaited son Samuel. Or the parable's widow, pestering the judge.

So, I latched onto this career vision and I had a tough time letting go. But looking back, it may have been the right time to voice a prayer of relinquishment.

WHAT IT IS

The dictionary says *relinquish* means to voluntarily cease to claim. To hand over willingly. To consider the situation, and make a decision to stop pushing forward.

Spiritually, relinquishment yields to circumstances as they are, with God as Overseer. When we relinquish, we agree to be satisfied. We agree to give up our quest for change. We agree to stop asking for what we assume is God's best will. We agree to be okay with what we can't fully grasp.

I don't understand it, but I accept it. Because I trust You, God, I'm okay with setting this request aside.

Jesus prayed a prayer of relinquishment in Gethsemane. He knew the burden of desperate prayer. And He knew about letting it go. Others in Scripture knew what relinquishment felt like, too, faithful Abraham relinquishing his plans for raising Isaac, guilty David relinquishing his infant son's life, teenage Mary relinquishing her known future.

Relinquishment is different from resignation.

Resignation hunkers down in fear and steels itself for the worst.

Relinquishment looks fully at the painful situation and releases demands, but clings to hope.

Relinquishment is bigger than surrender.

Surrender is stepping back, laying down weapons, and admitting the fight is bigger than you.

Relinquishment is letting go with expectation, pressing forward with a new vision.

WHEN TO DO IT

Sometimes the calendar or circumstances call for us to relinquish. The job is filled, we get past childbearing years, our ex remarries, the casket is closed. But other times, there is no resolution in this realm. And our tendency is to keep asking.

But perhaps the Spirit urges us differently sometimes.

Ecclesiastes tells us there is a time to give up, not on God, but on searching.

Searching for a wholeness, a healing, a homecoming.

Searching for the issue to be resolved our way.

Sometimes what we are pursuing is hurtful or destructive, even though it started out differently. Sometimes we have placed our identity in the idea of this pursuit, instead of in God. Sometimes where we are headed is simply outside of God's best for us, mysterious as it may seem.

Relinquishment is not an everyday prayer. It is not the first prayer we pray, but it might be the last. It comes only after we've petitioned tirelessly. We have to get to the point past desperation. We have to be prepared to give up the very thing we value most for God's greater planned good. When we do, a settled peace arrives as the desperation lifts.

From my journal just after my heart failure diagnosis:

We're nearing two weeks in ICU. Things continue to spin out of control so fast I am dizzy and heartbroken. My husband, not blunted by the gift of medication, is feeling the full force of this shocking situation. Tonight, he shared with me that as he was praying for my survival, he felt a certain peace that everything would be okay even if I wasn't healed. Let's just say it hit me wrong. I'm lying here fighting with everything I've got. And he's already giving up on me? I shot back at him, "I'm not gonna die!" I asked my husband to leave my room. Some disappointments don't allow room for company.

Turns out, as he usually is, my husband was way ahead of me in his spiritual expedition. He had already given the situation to God and taken his desires off the table. He had reached relinquishment. I think about that moment maybe more than any other during that harsh stretch of time. It made me a different kind of Christian. Less a Christ petitioner, more a Christ seeker.

WHY DO IT

When we find ourselves bent in two over the weight of our continuing request, we may be at the point of relinquishment. Once we get there, we can become more than okay with it.

We can reach a new level of intimacy with God.

Doug Groothius has nursed his wife (and his own war-torn faith) through the dark tunnel of dementia. He has reached relinquishment with her incurable disease. "Rather than feeling like I'm always beating God with my fists, now I feel more like I'm resting in His arms."

And given enough space, those arms can direct something bigger than our own request. Ann Voskamp advises, "Hold space for ways that are higher than yours, the ways of the One who never stops holding you."

Maybe the goal of prayer is not so much to gain control of God's hand, but to open up His arms with possibilities we can't even conceive. Though the decisions we make in prayer never change His love for us, they may be key to releasing the next part of His plan for us.

Writer Catherine Marshall says, "A demanding spirit, with self-will as the rudder, blocks prayer." God has never been in the business of overriding our free will, so until we lay that down, He may, by nature, remain silent or still. His best for us may remain untapped.

For those of us who take comfort in calling the shots, it's a challenging charge.

As difficult as it is, relinquishment runs deep in our faith. Setting aside self is the core of the gospel message. But that same gospel hinges on hope. So we know our acceptance of His sometimes-meandering way can never preclude ultimate hope. God's road never ends in disappointment.

GETTING OKAY WITH IT

We walked away from that two-fer job offer because it made no sense. We just couldn't get okay with it. But we held onto our dream for many years until we finally relinquished it. My husband and I never did open our own CPA firm. I switched careers (a couple of times) and he has been successful in accounting going another route.

But perhaps by not getting the jobs we wanted, God was laying the groundwork for me to survive the heart failure He saw coming long ago. I am grateful for the flood of care and support I've had on this unexpected path. Who knows, maybe I wouldn't have found it under the plan I was doggedly holding onto.

But the detour continues.

For full disclosure, I still pray every day for my heart to be healed. And, as you might expect, I pray hard. But, just as with that post-grad-school dream, it's possible that someday I may stop asking. At that point, I would fully anticipate something even better, as my request steps aside. Now, maybe for the first time, I can imagine my intense petition shifting one day to a prayer of relinquishment.

When that day comes, I hope I will finally be able to say, *Because of Him, I am more than okay with that.*

DAY 29

When God Disappoints

I shielded the California sun from my eyes for a glimpse as my son crossed the stage to receive his college diploma. Wearing my cardiac life vest, I didn't feel out of place as the camera-like device hanging around my neck looked like every other parent's equipment. My husband leaned toward me on the crowded bleachers. "Let's do this again in four years."

I nodded, but we both knew it was a long shot. A simple enough desire that seemed an impossible dream at that point. None of my doctors would have bet in our favor. My heart failure was just too advanced.

And yet, four years later we found ourselves living in the results of yesterday's prayers.

Sort of.

NOT LIKE WE HAD ENVISIONED

There was a reason my husband put a marker at four years. Our younger daughter had just been accepted to the same university and would be on track to graduate that year.

And miraculously, four years later, I was maintaining my permanently lowered heart function. But I was not in California. My family was not together. Graduation had been cancelled for containment of the pandemic. My heart ached at the disappointment of not being able to sit in those bleachers again like we'd prayed, and say, "Look! We did it!"

Originally, I just wanted to live long enough to see these kids of mine graduate. Still, I felt slighted. I had vowed to never get the device that now lives permanently inside my chest. My heart still isn't functioning as normal. I missed a ceremony I had hoped to attend.

Like so many times in my life, prayers have been answered but I don't recognize them when they're at my door. They don't look like I envisioned, so I assume God blew me off. I'm not the first to harbor grandiose hopes that didn't perfectly align with God's eventual handiwork. I'm not the first to feel disappointed by God.

When Jesus rode into Jerusalem on Palm Sunday, the people who had seen His miracles and anticipated His prophesied appearance were expecting a deliverance from the Roman Empire. They had their own ideas of what that would entail. But the fulfilled promise ended up looking very different. The construction of His kingdom took a path through an unbelievable crucifixion by way of a donkey of peace rather than a horse of war.

Jesus didn't do what people expected, but instead, what He promised.

And that's always been His way.

EXPECTED vs PROMISED

At one time, my familiar kitchen table was covered with a painful mix of hospital floral arrangements, mysterious prescription bottles, a framed prayer chain, and a dreadful binder.

From my journal a few months after my diagnosis:

It's on the kitchen table next to my newly acquired collection of high-powered prescription meds. The spine in harsh dark letters shouting "End of Life Care." It has been there so long I'm not seeing it anymore. The shock factor has worn off. I wonder what to do with it. Should I leave it out in case we need it? Should I put it on the coffee table next to the family photo album and our monthly magazines?

"Though I walk through the valley of the valley of the shadow of death, You are with me..." I keep rereading that psalm and hoping it's true.

And then a journal entry more than a year later:

Today, despite not being healed, I decided to finally give myself per-

mission to stop waiting to die and start to live again. I took that hospice binder off the kitchen table and put it in a file. One day I might need it. But today is not that day.

The day I filed that binder away, I realized God's promise was fulfilled. He walked with me *through* the dark valley and continues there with me. And yet, every time I tell my story, I forget about that part. Because I envisioned something totally different. I expected Him to take me *out of* the valley.

Jesus doesn't promise an easy or even a resolved life.

We can't reshape God's promises into our expectations. But like the palm-waving crowd, we do.

The recent pandemic season and my own illness have been teaching me something my entire faith life could not. *Some of our promise-backed prayers will always seem unanswered. Because, in our lifetime, the completion of His promises often won't look like we expect.*

And that may be by design.

WAIT FOR IT

We live in a world where parents bury children, innocent people are punished, families desert us, and stories don't end in the way, or the time, we prayed.

It is human to yearn for every request to be met, for all of our expectations to be fulfilled. But it is a faithful person's challenge to understand this: Completion can never be achieved here. Not out of cruelty or punishment. Quite the opposite. It is our tether to eternity. It is our tie to Him.

And sometimes that tie feels like waiting.

Many of us waited through the pandemic for a memorial service or a wedding that should have taken place months earlier. I waited for the graduation ceremony that happened later the following year. I'm still waiting for the full healing that may never come. I wanted clearance to visit my parents before Dad entered hospice care, and I want a lapful of grandchildren someday.

All of that is expected, none of it is promised.

God owns tomorrow, I simply steward today.

And we are bound together by the tension of this working, waiting relationship.

One day when I pull out that hospice binder because I need a phone number or next steps, I will remember something my husband told me, *I am trading what I can't keep for something I can never lose.*

Meanwhile, the unmet expectation, the waiting, is pulling me toward Him and that ultimate promise.

HOPE IS LIVING A FUTURE PROMISE

We can't expect what God never promised, but we can always expect what He did.

He doesn't promise to save us from life's suffering, but He does promise to use our suffering to eventually produce hope: "[S]uffering produces perseverance; perseverance, character; and character, hope" (Romans 5:3–4 NIV).

And that's exactly how that binder left the kitchen table.

Author Jay Wolf wrote, "Hope is a future promise lived out in the present." God used my suffering to instill hope in His eternal healing, and I started to live the coming promise.

Four-year-old prayers were eventually answered, but they didn't look like I thought they would. The graduation ceremonies were abbreviated and by invitation only. I didn't meet my daughter's professors or tour her campus. Most of her friends didn't return for their delayed pomp and circumstance. Her grandparents passed away in the year between the original date and the rescheduled one. I didn't escape my implanted device. I haven't been healed from my disease.

But I am still alive. My daughter graduated and was accepted into a graduate program a bit closer to home. God is good, and He answers prayers. And Hope is alive at our house.

Even when He rides in on a donkey.

Even when disease and disappointment linger.

Even when the fulfillment of His promise looks nothing like we expected.

DAY 30

Trust Enough to Surrender

Let go! Let go!"

Our twenty-something-aged friends yelled in unison from the swollen river's bank, some reaching a panicked tone. The canoe my thrill-seeking husband and I were floating in had taken a corner a little fast and capsized. He immediately let go, went under, and then popped up on the far side of a downed branch. I, on the other hand, was holding tightly to said branch as the sideways canoe banged repeatedly into my torso.

Petrified and unwilling to release my grip on that tree, I clung desperately for several minutes. My husband pleaded; my friends urged. I had my reasons for not letting go. I didn't trust my swimming ability. I was wearing contact lenses (the kind you replaced once a year). I didn't want to get my freshly permed late-1980s hair wet.

But more than anything, I refused to release my last shred of control.

Finally, after I could no longer hold myself up, I let go, still terrified I would drown in the fast-moving water or get tangled in more branches under the canoe. Amazingly, I went under and popped up right about where my husband had.

When my ears cleared, I could hear everyone clapping.

And I could feel my husband's familiar arms securely around me.

I was safe even in the middle of the rapid river.

But first, I had to let go.

A DESIRE TO KEEP FIGHTING

Somehow, in all of life, continuing the struggle often seems easier to do.

When I got bad news about my heart function at one early check-up, my first instinct was to draw the battle lines and rally the troops. I was primed for a fight.

From my journal:

At least we don't have to fight the battle that my decrease could be due to inadequate care since Cleveland Clinic is the world's heart authority. But there is still plenty of struggle. With this chronic, progressive disease, I'm winning when I can slow it down, or hold it steady. The reality is, right now I'm losing. I'm going to double down on low sodium, rest, and walking my daily 10,000 steps until I return to Cleveland in a few weeks. At least I'll be doing my part to get my life back.

But the truth is, after years in the trenches, this warrior is weary. (Or as we are becoming accustomed to saying in our house, "Momma is tired.")

When we're in a perpetual fight with chronic illness or creditors or co-dependent children, we wear ourselves out. The ongoing burden becomes too heavy to carry. But the fight, the burden, was never meant to be ours.

THE BATTLE IS HIS

"The Lord will fight for you; you need only to be still" (Exodus 14:14 NIV).

It seems the striving part for me comes naturally. Sometimes I feel like I've been fighting all my life. (My husband and my mother have both used the word *stubborn*.) Fighting for a ranking in grad school, a position at work. Fighting deadlines or budgets or decisions I have no real control over, or just plain injustice. And in all that struggle I have learned something.

At some point, you have to let go of the fight.

Because sometimes to win, you have to surrender.

I have practiced some letting go—remnants of time or money or possessions. Even in the canoe fiasco, I released my grip on our battered garage sale cooler (after some coaxing), not knowing if it would end up with a new family downstream. I am good at surrendering what I want to surrender. Which, in the end, is no surrender at all.

God wants us to yield to His all-encompassing plan, to the complete package.

Total surrender is a difficult concept for a fighter. I resist surgery and airplane travel and even pedicures, because giving up that much control is painful and risky. And often difficult to rationalize.

The completely human part of Jesus's nature questioned God's plan at Gethsemane: "Going a little ahead, he fell on his face, praying, 'My Father, if there is any way, get me out of this. But please, not what I want. You, what do *you* want?'" (Matthew 26:39 MSG).

Even in the suffering, Jesus knew how to feel the safety of the Father's arms. To become part of His plan, we have to let go of ours.

A NEW LOOK AT SURRENDER

We have to surrender to the One who has always been fighting on our side. The One who has already won. It should be an easy sell. The problem is, fighters are wired to resist surrender.

But I've been learning to see surrender in a new light.

Surrender is not a passive giving in, but an active going on.

Surrender is not a defeat, but a detour from our own plan.

Surrender is not giving up, it's giving it over…to Someone stronger.

Instead of limiting our options or confining us, surrender breaks open God's glorious potential for our lives. The active trust of surrender propels us into God's story.

Early on when my health canoe capsized, I clung to a different branch—the outcome. The water of trouble pulled hard, threatening to drag me under. But as Eckhart Tolle says, "It is an act of far greater power to let something go than to hold onto it."

What Tolle may not have realized is the power we tap into is from God.

THE BEST ENDING

Rather than the outcome, I should have been clinging to God, trusting Him for the end of the story.

As with Moses's staff-turned-snake, we first have to lay down what's in our hand—we have to surrender our own strength to gain His. We must do what we can, but leave the final result in God's hands.

In doing this, we begin to realize what God wanted us to know all along. The outcome doesn't depend on our power or ability, but His.

When I finally let go of that branch on our ill-fated canoe trip, it was one of the most difficult things I'd done in my twenty-five years of life. Decades later, as the rushing waters of heart failure have swept in, I've had to relearn how to let go.

So, what is the new plan, post-heart-failure diagnosis? That's just it. I don't know. And I get frustrated when it seems the doctors don't know either. But the Holy Spirit is laboring to help me find peace even without answers.

A complete surrender also requires that.

And I have a feeling when I get enough courage to let go of that branch, He'll be right there to catch me.

DAY 31

Sitting on the Bus

When we were growing up on the farm, for reasons too complicated and too political for my six-year-old mind, the school bus picked my siblings and me up and dropped us off a half mile from our home at the intersection of four wheat fields.

Usually, Mom drove us up to the corner a tad early because the bus driver was cranky and didn't like to be kept waiting. In fact, several mornings the bus left without us because I forgot a book and would have to run back into the house before driving up to the corner. The bus driver was also notorious for kicking us out at the end of the day if Mom wasn't there to meet the bus. My siblings and I then walked home on the busy blacktop road.

One day in first grade, I was on the bus by myself since my older brother and sister had after school activities. When we pulled into the half-mile spot, my mother was not there. It was frigid and windy and starting to spit ice. The weather had made a dramatic change during that early spring day. And in the crazy rush of the morning, I had forgotten my coat.

I remember shooting a glance at the driver, trying to read her mood. I felt myself coming undone. *Would she make me walk by myself?* I pressed my face to the fogged window, imagining every millisecond that Mom's avocado-colored Pontiac would appear.

Where could she be?

WHEN GOD SEEMS LATE

The same question arises in our faith journey. *Why isn't God showing up?* And sometimes in the excruciating waiting, we begin to question the nature of God and His timing.

Jesus waited two days before returning to ill Lazarus. When He did arrive, it seemed obviously too late. His friend had already died.

Author of *When Life and Beliefs Collide*, Carolyn Custis James explains, "Every grief is two-dimensional—the loss itself, along with the nagging thought that it could have been prevented if only God had acted."

If only He had acted in time. In *our* time.

If only You had been here, my brother, my career, my dream, my marriage, would not have died. Where were You? What took You so long? Have You not been listening to my cries?

Early in my diagnosis, I struggled with how to connect my beliefs about God with what was happening in my life. Or more accurately, with what wasn't happening.

Almost immediately, I became obsessed with being healed. Every day and every thought centered around meds and side effects, diet and exercise, rest and research. We had done everything the doctors had asked and everything we could think of spiritually. My six-year-old face was pressed against the foggy window for sixteen months.

But God did not appear. Or at least healing didn't.

SHIFTING FOCUS

Some days I miss the blissful, hazy comprehension of childhood. Back then, I knew enough to know I didn't know. And I accepted that. Lately, I've been trying to revive this childlike trust that Jesus admired. Such unassuming faith is always what sustains us in our most desperate times, when our reasoning fails us, when we can't possibly understand what's happening.

Simply taking God at His Word. "I am with you always, to the end of the age" (Matthew 28:20b ESV).

On that bus, I was thinking about my mother and how much I loved her. How I had always depended on her. How she was worthy of my faith in her.

Yet, for months in my adult health journey, I was focused on the outcome instead of on God. Without realizing it, I had made my problem bigger than my God.

I made this journal entry on Easter Sunday, one year to the day before my heart function ever measurably improved:

At church I had to face all the people who had been praying for me for four months. Most already knew the bad news we got in Cleveland and just wanted to be supportive. I tried to hold it together but wasn't 100 percent successful. Something about a sympathetic hug or smile was breaking my heart. They wanted it as much as I did, and I wanted so much to celebrate a victory today. Maybe mostly for them. I spent a good deal of the service biting my bottom lip to hold back the tears. I told my husband later that I don't even know if what I'm truly wanting is to be healed. I just want to see His hand move. For all of us.

I would live another full year before beginning to understand the waiting. I didn't realize it then, but waiting was starting to transform me. My focus was shifting from the result to Him. When the dust of desperate pleading cleared, I just wanted God's undeniable presence. I wanted Him to be real.

WAITING GIVES PERSPECTIVE

In the waiting, we begin to realize what we truly desire, what we're really waiting for is Him.

In waiting for Jesus, Lazarus's sister Martha learned her true faith was in Him rather than in the temporary physical help He could provide. She ran to Jesus as He approached their home, even though her brother did not survive. Even though she didn't yet understand why He would be so obviously late.

During those tense moments waiting in the bus with the scary bus driver, I knew with every fiber of my nervous being that Mom was on her way. And watching the ice collect on the bus windows, I recounted reasons I was thankful to have her in my life.

After what seemed hours, Mom's car pulled in and I hurried off the bus. Trying to walk too fast to hear the driver threaten, "Next time, if you-ens don't have a ride, I gotta leave!" Mom had arrived just in time, and her faithfulness demonstrated I could depend on her. But I wouldn't have realized it without the wait.

One of my biggest lessons from heart failure: Waiting builds dependency on God.

When God says *Wait*, He is saying, *Cling to Me*. Rather than on an outcome or a result. He puts Himself above the request. Which helps us see He is our only lasting hope.

The most difficult and most important spiritual work of any life will happen in the waiting. Sitting on that bus.

And sometimes that takes more time than we'd like.

DAY 32

Not What We Expected

We said goodbye in the middle of a bizarre autumn cold snap.

It should have been in the high sixties that day. But it wasn't.

Snow fell like grace in the October wheatfields as we buried my mother. A strange blanket of comfort, as if God was saying, *Unexpected things happen, but it doesn't mean I'm not in control. It actually means, "I Am." Like manna raining down from heaven.*

For the wandering Israelites and for my wounded family, it wasn't what we wanted or expected. It's not what we petitioned or prayed for. It's not what those with God-given talents and abilities predicted.

Mom lived longer than most. I want to be good with it. I want to tie it up with a big bow. But I'm struggling. Before Dad lost his battle with cancer, she was vibrant and lively. We were planning for her next phase, and many more years. Then less than four months later, with no warning and no final words, we lost her.

GOD OF THE UNEXPECTED

As much as I want a full justification (written, preferably), I feel sure I'm not getting one.

And there's good reason why. He's good at being God. And, as Anne Lamott says, "A good name for God is 'Not Me.'"

Because my mind could never comprehend His perfect plan.

Just like my toddler son's brain couldn't wrap around why I had to take away all his "bobs." (Those pacifiers would not be a good look in grad school.) Trying to walk my tiny boy through the reasoning would have been pointless.

It's possible that, even as adults, we don't recognize God's best for us because we can't recognize our own deepest need. So the unexpected often feels confusing.

"God doesn't owe us an explanation every time He does something we don't understand." —Bob Goff

Our confusion is tempered by this: From the desert manna to Sarah's child to a donkey-riding King, *not what we expected* is how our God works. And it's how He loves.

Despite my limited understanding, I live every day bound tight in this unpredictable love. And whether you know it or not, so do you.

DISAPPOINTMENT HAPPENS

We all carry unmet expectations. Career climbs or relationship resolutions or illness eradications. Worthy ideas we were sure God would approve of and support. But somehow, He didn't.

Like my mother holding a grandchild of mine. Or my own heart function being restored.

These unmet expectations create disappointment, then disappointment can cause grumbling. And it's not just the big things.

From my journal:

The chronic part of this illness is wearing thin on me. Somehow, I just didn't expect it to last this long. All my life I've been a stomach sleeper. Even through all three pregnancies, I insisted. Now, with the special ICD implanted so close to the surface of the skin on my left chest, I can't. It's the right side or the back, which means lots of tossing and turning, night after night.

How quickly I forgot about my earlier miracle. The enlarged heart everyone else had given up on, somehow still beating.

Surely the Israelites could relate. They lost their love for the life-sustaining manna and begged for something better. Just one chapter removed from the miraculous Red Sea parting, they expected God to move bodies of water to accommodate them. I often only look for God where I saw Him last too. He had so recently scaffolded my own failing health I was sure He'd be right there to do the same for Mom.

Though this God is not predictable, His people can be. Notorious for grumbling, expecting a quick and straight route to the Promised Land. But God builds in time and detours to teach us daily dependence and proven protection.

My mother understood this. I never knew her to express disappointment in her God. She had a survival grit inside that tiny frame. And I saw her deep faith give God space to work through life's daily difficulties and unmet expectations.

RELEASING OUR EXPECTATIONS

As vivid an example as I had in Mom, it took heart failure to tutor me firsthand on releasing expectations. I'm still struggling to apply the lessons to losses I've suffered since:

I've learned I can release my expectations into the hands of a God who cares, but often doesn't give me what I want.

I've learned that when I don't understand, I can still trust in His sovereignty. That doesn't make me a hypocrite or shallow or irrational. It makes me human. It makes me a believer.

I've learned I can lay His past faithfulness over the places I still don't have answers. Because He's never promised to be a God of the expected.

I've learned I can lament that to be in this world is to have precious little control over my life.

I've learned that faith cannot cure a body from being human, and I should stop expecting it to.

I've learned that if my life could be predicted by mathematical models and scientific projections, I wouldn't need Him. And the intimacy of prayer would be meaningless.

I've learned this is a God who doesn't want to be explained away, but rather, invited in.

"And He said, My Presence will go *with you*" (Exodus 33:14 NKJV).

God's presence again came in a form I hadn't anticipated. Even as we pulled up to the mere handful of funeral home chairs and empty graveside parking, I remembered my longtime friends who had driven ten hours through the unpredicted ice the day before. I wasn't expecting them either.

THE SILENT TREATMENT

As my weak heart reminds me daily, I am much closer to the end of this journey than I am the beginning, and most days I still have more questions than answers. So I keep asking. The Israelites learned, too, the key is to never stop talking to Him along the way, even when that communication sounds more like grumbles and complaints. Even when all we can do is ask, *Why*?

Shivering next to Mom's casket, I glanced at Dad's grave with fresh dirt still on top. I wanted to give God the silent treatment. This God I had known so long refused to be who I thought I needed: a wish-granter, a people-pleaser, a God of the expected.

But just as with my parents in high school, I couldn't pull off the silent treatment to God for long. Our love had too much history.

Moses and his people were living on the other, more foggy, side of the resurrection. We are blessed to already know the end of the Big Story. We just don't know how our individual chapter will unfold, though we expect certain things by reading everyone else's chapter. As Easter weekend reminds us, even when our human expectations are crushed and our worst fears our realized, it is not the end in God's narrative.

Mom signed a DNR and told my brother the day she died she was ready whenever that time came. I don't think she was expecting it so soon either.

Following the service, we stood at my mother's grave longer than we should have in those icy conditions. We couldn't bear the thought of leaving her alone in the frozen ground. Somewhere she'd never leave any of us.

But as I climbed into the warm car, I realized she wasn't alone.

And I knew she never expected to be.

DAY 33

In Between

I knew the look on my husband's face as he started turning his pockets inside out.

Thinking about breaking for lunch from the long theme park lines, he made the realization.

Our keys were missing. And not just our hotel key.

It was an Airbnb key (and a remote gate key) along with the rental car key. After a few hours retracing our steps, scouring lost and found, then combing through attraction queues, ride seats, and auditoriums, we began to add up the worst-case scenario.

Our Airbnb host said we would have to pay for a new house key and if the old key wasn't found, to have the lock changed on the house. Also, the gate would need to be rekeyed. The car's smart key was not cheap, either, and we would have to get the car towed from the Universal parking lot back to the Hertz office. Not to mention the Ubers to get around and back to the airport. In Southern California, we were easily looking at four figures to get out of this mess.

We knew we would eventually get back home, with an interesting story to tell. But we had no idea what would unfold in the interim. And the prospects of what might happen had us fretting a bit.

For someone who should have a punch card with Pop-A-Lock, it was a familiar feeling.

EMBRACING THE TENSION

It was not so much the expense of the worst case; it was that unknown period. Suspended in limbo for most of the day, not knowing whether to be delightfully carefree or deeply concerned. We tried to have a good time, but we kept running to the front of the massive park to check lost and found. A dark cloud stalked our family the rest of the day.

Ruth experienced a much deeper, darker gray space: the loss of her husband and father-in-law, her home in Moab, her way of life. On a smaller scale, I've felt it, too, with my heart failure battle.

As God-followers, we are charged to live the story, trusting Him to finish it. And sometimes that means hanging out for a while in between, in *liminal space.*

Liminal space is the space between two points of existence.

Physically, these spaces might be stairwells, elevators, hallways, parking lots.

Nonphysical liminal spaces could be the space between

- losing a job and finding a new one,
- leaving a home and settling into another home,
- ending a relationship and starting another,
- being diagnosed and being healed.

We are familiar with the place we are leaving, and we can envision where we will end up. Liminal space is the transition, a place of waiting. It's after God shuts one door and before He opens another—the hellish hallway.

Above all, liminal space is a place of not knowing. It's where faith lives.

Anytime we experience loss, we enter liminal space, the tension between the familiar and the foreign. God's design is that the old is often not immediately followed by the new. He builds in a buffer to prepare our hearts.

I'm sure Ruth was ready to get on with her life, to skip the gray—the gleaning, and the growing.

Most of my Type-A life I've seen liminal space as wimpy, wavering, wasted. But I'm learning to look at those in-betweens differently now.

GOD'S TRANSFORMATIONAL WORK

My husband and I enjoy a good Netflix series. It all started with *Stranger Things*. We didn't realize at first how much of that story unfolded in the alternate reality, the "Upside-Down." If I could write a spiritual sequel to *Stranger Things*, I'd include the "In-Between" in place of the "Upside-Down." It's where the most important part of our Christ-following story unfolds.

Spiritually, liminal space is a gift that slows the film reel, allowing transformation to occur. A space where we grow in patience and other spiritual fruits, where we get to know God better and trust Him more. The place where we become closer to Him than we ever thought possible on the shores of certainty. We eventually realize that the tension of the unknown is far better than life alone.

And in-between is the only space where a new reality can be born. Author and theologian Richard Rohr describes this sacred space "where the old world is able to fall apart, and a bigger world is revealed."

In Ruth's liminal space, she had an opportunity to solidify her commitment to Naomi. This is exactly what Boaz noticed and loved about Ruth. And by faithfully leaning into that in-between, Ruth married Boaz, and their son was born into the lineage of Jesus.

And there were many others.

Gethsemane was liminal space. So was the Israelites' desert. And Paul's prison. Also, Miriam placing baby brother Moses in the Nile, and Abraham placing hope in God's ancestral promise. We are blessed to see more than just the in-between of those stories.

The same God is still in the business of finishing stories today.

From my journal:

In two months, we will go back to Cleveland Clinic. We know the journey well. Physically, we have our usual stops, and medically, we've got the routine down. What we don't know is the part of the story we're living right now, in these slow-motion months while we are between visits. I don't know if I'm at the end of something (being a "high-functioning" heart failure patient) and at the beginning of something else (becoming a transplant patient). Or still squarely in between.

We have lived most of the last years in this limbo.

I have often wondered why the nurses and doctors who first treated me would leave my room in tears. They saw so many patients, many suffering more or closer to death than I was. I realize now that they were crying about something I didn't even know to mourn yet, more of a living loss. Heart failure, with its unspecific prognosis, had ushered me into a sort of gray space for the rest of my life. Now all I can do is live my best story, to make sure these middle chapters aren't wasted. And wait to see what God does next.

In its original Latin, *liminal* means *threshold, the point of entry, the beginning.*

That same word, that same space, that we can experience as a dark, silent bunker, can also be a brink. Faith requires that we see liminal space not as a holding cell, but as a threshold with a unique view of what God has next for us in His story.

THE OTHER SIDE OF UNCERTAINTY

Some responsible soul turned in our keys to lost and found the next day. They fell out of my husband's pocket on the *Harry Potter and the Forbidden Journey* ride. (He still asserts that ride was worth all the stress.)

We were spared the worst of our fears, as we so often are in this life.

Still, like the theme park fiasco and Ruth's hazy future, right now, I am living in liminal space.

In between.

On the threshold.

Maybe you are too. Mourning a loss, gleaning in foreign fields, waiting for healing. Know that you're not forgotten in your liminal space.

Because our God has a perfect ending in mind.

For every story.

DAY 34

Mid-race Joy

It was the perfect sunny day in April to watch my first Boston Marathon.

I left our Airbnb early with a plan. I had mapped out the subway stops, then waited my turn at the front of the temporary railing along Boylston Street. I was several blocks from the race's end at Copley Square where it was only about ten people deep. I didn't have a chance getting this close to the course near the finish line, so I was thrilled to find this mid-race spot.

The marathon app let me track my husband along his run. Over the next two hours, I slowly made my way to the barrier as spectators left. I was set in front and ready well before he was scheduled to make the corner and turn onto Boylston. I knew to look for a bright orange singlet. My husband had no idea I would score a front-row vantage point among over a million ardent enthusiasts.

As he approached my point on the course, other runners were seeing their families along the fence and running over to them, hugging them, kissing them, high-fiving them. I recruited a spectator next to me to take our picture when my husband came to the rail. When I finally spotted him, I started yelling his name. I jumped up and down. Leaning over the railing, I waved my arms like I was herding raging cattle, flapping the makeshift sign someone had handed me. The guy next to me offered to help yell louder. Soon a small group joined in.

My husband never even glanced in my direction.

He ran right past...with a big smile on his face.

THE BEST PLACE FOR A CELEBRATION

Defeated, I relinquished my coveted position to someone else's family fan club waiting behind me.

Once we were finally reunited on the other side of the finish line, I questioned him about the brush-off at the barricade. My husband said, "I thought I heard my name, but I don't know anyone else here, and I assumed you were staying in the room. Besides, it sounded like a man's voice, so I figured it couldn't be me they were yelling for."

After a bit more probing, he admitted he had convinced himself that since the probability of it being me yelling at the fence was very small, he should keep on running to maintain his time. We could always celebrate together later.

Although I support my husband's love for running, as a nonrunner, I'm usually not jazzed by the associated sport talk. But after this extended run with heart failure, I've started noticing something about prolonged challenges: Somewhere in the middle is the best place to celebrate.

Highly trained long-distance runners (like my husband) can hit a point several miles in where a long race starts getting easier. This "runner's high" is a feeling of extreme well-being when endorphins, dopamine, and other biochemical substances are released in the body.

Chronic illness fighters know the drill of the long course. Storm clouds continually darken and threaten, questions often nag, pain still visits. Wading through a stagnant pandemic, a drawn-out divorce, or prolonged unemployment, most of us can relate. Yet many have found the runner's high, a sort of "mid-race joy." And it's deeper and richer than situational happiness.

The apostle Paul often used race metaphors in his Spirit-led writing. During his mid-race prison term, Paul knew "the infinite value of knowing Christ Jesus" (Philippians 3:8 NLT). Paul knew how to find deep joy within the long challenges of life.

MEANINGFUL MID-RACE WORSHIP

I have a bad habit of waiting to the end, the sure last chapter, to let down my guard and rejoice. (I'm way worse than my husband.) But that's an inconvenient and sobering stance to take with heart failure and in life.

Here's what I'm learning: It's okay to celebrate in the middle of a crisis. In fact, it's necessary. And we are not discounting the world's suffering, or our personal pain if we do. As Jennie Allen says, "We can observe our suffering without being overtaken by our suffering."

Mid-race joy is a form of worship—showing love to a God who will never abandon us and recognizing this in the messy middle when it seems He still could.

Lifting up God is the most powerful experience, not when we get what we have asked for, but maybe most purely when we don't. It is more honest and real to honor God before everything comes together, while it still feels like it's falling apart. That way we are honoring Him and not the result.

Joy is possible and necessary in the middle because that's the only place true worship happens. Perhaps our race is dragging on "that we might not rely on ourselves but on God" (2 Corinthians 1:9b NIV). It's where Paul began writing the book that talks so much about running the good race.

When this race is all over, I want to remember that I needed Him just as desperately on my best day as I did on my worst.

He is as faithful and real in the middle as He is at the end. The middle is the tough part, though. It's where jobs are uncertain, marriages teeter, healings haven't happened. The middle doesn't have the optimism of the beginning or the thrill of the end. But the middle is where every race is won. Because it's where the story unfolds. It's where life is lived.

As Katherine Wolf describes in *Suffer Strong*, "Celebration can be an act of worship and an act of hope and perhaps, in a way, an act of joyful rebellion against fear."

Mid-race joy is an act of celebrating the life we have and accepting whatever is ahead that we cannot see. The dark middle days are where we trust He's not just a Healer, He's a Resurrector.

And the joy comes in knowing that even when every fiber seems to be coming undone, when every muscle is out of energy and the path ahead seems impossibly long, we are never left to run the race alone.

AN UNKNOWN MIDDLE, A KNOWN END

The hard part about endurance races in life is that, unlike a true marathon, we don't always know how long a race we're in for. And sometimes we misjudge it.

From my journal sixteen months into my disease:

We had a checkup at Cleveland Clinic today to determine if the pacemaker/defibrillator that was installed in August had improved my heart function. The doctors were not optimistic. They expected maybe, at best, a five-point bump due to the advanced stage of my heart failure. But they obviously did not account for the power of prayer to move God's hand. Unbelievably, after more than a year with no progress, my heart function doubled from 12 percent to 25 percent. The doctor cried. My husband and I cried. My cardiologist in Cleveland said I am no longer her most critical patient. Evelina, the sonographer that we have formed a relationship with over the past year, called me Cleveland Clinic's "miracle woman."

I thought I was nearing the end, but I am, even years later, still mid-race on this chronic disease.

Much of any life can feel like a marathon with no finish line in sight. And even as believers, we struggle. Living in the shadow of faith in this mundane, maniacal middle—that is our challenging charge as Christians.

Marathons are difficult, even for the trained athlete. Also hard are infertility, finances, relationships, life this side of eternity.

But our mid-race joy boldly echoes a truth along our uncharted territory, *Although we don't know the entire course, we know how it ends.*

My husband ran a personal best at the Boston Marathon that year. And he was in the top 30 percent overall. Pretty impressive for a first-timer at the legendary race. And who knows? A visit to the fence might have wrecked his rhythm or concentration or pace. We still laugh about that, lamenting that we never got the picture I had meticulously planned for.

Knowing my husband's love for the sport and his years-long desire to compete there, he was rejoicing as he passed me, striding down Boylston toward the Boston Marathon finish line. He had his eyes on the prize, like he always has in his Christian race.

And as we all should do in the long course, he actually was celebrating mid-race.

It just looked a little different than I had planned.

DAY 35

Making Mistakes

I've been through the events in my mind for years, trying to nail down how it could have happened. This is my best guess.

One Saturday pre-chronic-illness, I walked into the kitchen to take my once-a-week bone density pill. As I unwrapped my pill, the phone rang. I answered the landline, my mother and I talked as I stood tethered to the wall. Our conversation reminded me that it was the first of the month, time for my dog's heartworm medication. After hanging up, I found her pill, and dug into the fridge for the requisite cheese to wrap it in. My dog Mocha gulped it down. Then, realizing I never took my own pill, I reached for the remaining pill on the counter.

It wasn't mine.

I looked at my eight-pound dog and panicked. I called the emergency vet line and was met with a barrage of questions.

Receptionist: *Yes, that would be toxic for dogs. How did the dog get your pill?*

Me: *I gave it to her…accidentally.*

Receptionist: *That's strange because dogs usually won't eat human medication due to the smell.*

Me: *I wrapped it in cheese.*

(Prolonged silence on the other end as I realized how that sounded. And as they considered whether they should call the ASPCA.)

Let's just say I had some explaining to do, with the receptionist and with my nine-year-old daughter who came on the scene in time to see me purposefully shaking our miniature dachshund, Etch-a-Sketch style, per the vet's instructions.

1. Pry open the dog's mouth and pour in "a lot of" hydrogen peroxide.
2. Shake *the dog* vigorously until foam comes out of her mouth.
3. She will vomit several times over the next few hours.
4. You will have to make sure the pill eventually comes up.

This mistake did not make me Mother of the Year with my daughter or with my dog.

AVOIDING MISTAKES

If you're like me, you've spent a good chunk of your life avoiding such notable mistakes. (Because, among other reasons, kids tend to tell and retell certain incriminating ones.) Honestly, all my life I had been subtly erecting an identity on being right. I wish I'd realized long ago that somehow the brokenness seems to find us anyway. Not always by our design, sometimes just by circumstance.

And other times, by ignoring a problem.

Though I had no risk factors and no family history, I had early warning signs of heart failure: shortness of breath, inability to exercise, fatigue. For years, my family urged me to go to the doctor. I wish I could tell you I listened to them, that I swallowed my middle-aged pride, that I went to my trusted family physician, that I shared completely and honestly in annual exams. I did none of those things. And that error damaged my heart and shortened my life.

MISTAKES CAN BE VALUABLE

Living with that mistake (which, conveniently, has the word *failure* built right in), has taught me another valuable lesson: Faults can sometimes provide an unrivaled opportunity. Psychologists and social researchers have found that mistakes eventually make us safer, braver, stronger. Once we recover and do a correction of errors, we learn what *not* to do, how to be resilient, and ways to survive future blows.

Author Kathryn Schulz wrote in her book *Being Wrong*, "It is ultimately wrongness, not rightness, that can teach us who we are."

And I'd add, *Whose* we are.

Are we alone in this mistake-prone venture?

Or do we belong to Someone who's in control, despite our errors?

Our mistakes reveal our soul-need for God.

While mistakes don't define our identity, they do lay a foundation for the only relationship that should. Mistakes make us dependent on Him. It is our very imperfection that brings us to the cross. This mindset removes the burden of faults from our days and from our destiny. We recovering perfectionists need to continually remind ourselves: "God's 'well done' says less about the worth of our works than about the wonder of his mercy." —Scott Hubbard

THE OPPOSITE OF WHAT SHOULD BE

Weighed by the metric of mercy, grace makes mistakes into majesty.

Because grace is the opposite of what is logical—the opposite of what *should be.*

When Jonah ran from God, when he chose not to do what he should have done, God had a fish swallow him. But Jonah did not die. In fact, he lived because of that. The fish, rather than devouring him, saved him from drowning. Maybe what Jonah learned best that day was this: *When God is involved, salvation can look like not being consumed by that which should consume you.*

An early taste of grace.

Like me, Jonah spent years running. God used Jonah's mistake to save Nineveh, and ultimately, to save Jonah from himself. And the very disease that should have consumed me has, in many ways, saved me too. From my journal:

Over the past several years, I have felt my world closing in. Options, time, energy, the kids leaving the nest, fewer outside activities. The realm I operate in has definitely narrowed. Mostly out of necessity. But it hasn't affected me like I would have suspected. If I had looked into a crystal ball twenty or even ten years ago, I would have been terrified of the reality I'm living right now. But it's just the opposite. I have peace. And I have discovered a strangely mended purpose.

BETTER BROKEN

Kintsugi is the Japanese art of repairing broken pottery in a unique way. Instead of making the breaks less visible, instead of trying to mend the piece as if it had never been broken, this art form exalts the breaks. The pottery is restored with lacquer and the cracks are dusted with gold. The result is stunning and unique, the opposite of a useless, broken vessel.

In much the same way, our mistakes create space for grace.

As Donald Miller wrote, "Grace only sticks to our imperfections."

Decades ago, I wouldn't have believed it. We are more beautiful and useful in His kingdom, with imperfections, with our breaking points defined, our past mistakes highlighted. In the Father's careful Hands, a painful reality will one day become so much more than what it seemed.

We mistake-averse believers must know the only way we can stop the mistakes is to stop living. But we also know a God with a pretty impressive résumé of turning broken into beautiful—doubt to truth, darkness to light, death to life. He'll do the same for your secret addiction, your financial faux pas, even your parenting blunders (pets and people).

His touch has created the opposite of what *should be*. Disobedient Jonah survived; my post-diagnosis faith is thriving. My daughter actually does call me for advice.

As for my dog, the trauma of the pill incident should have made her avoid me at all cost. But just the opposite. She forgave me. Not right away, but almost a decade later she snuggled next to me every day through the early shock of heart failure. Somehow, she knew something about grace.

I'm not who I was before.

In many ways, as my five-year prognosis fades further away in the rearview mirror, I'm just the opposite.

A younger me was trying to substitute my own *rightness* for His.

I'm a bit more careful doling out medications now that I take so many. Mocha has passed away (from unrelated causes), but a new dog has taken her place. I've made a few mistakes with her as well, just like I did raising my children. Among others, my family will always remember that pill incident.

In the most important ways, I'm better now than I was then.

Not because I've overcome my imperfections, but because I've embraced their cure.

I've found that accepting grace overshadows the fear of failure.

And, in the grip of that grace, I'm watching my mended life become the opposite of what it really should be.

DAY 36

Parented by Porch Light

Oh no, the light is out. I'm in hot water.

Rolling onto the crunchy gravel drive long past my high school curfew, something seemed off. The familiar porch light that was always on until our last family member was safely inside, was dark. Either there had been a family emergency and they'd forgotten about me, or they hadn't forgotten about me and I *was* the family emergency.

The porch light shone in contrast to much of our frugal farm ways. Mom washed and reused every plastic bag and container that entered our house. Windows were open more than the air conditioner was on, and lights were often switched off before I had even left a room.

But one light my parents were generous with was the porch light.

Whether arriving home from late ballgames, harvest breakdowns, or weekend debate tournaments, that light was always on. Even most times when I blew past my curfew, it was still mercifully lit outside our brick ranch house in the country.

It's different arriving "home" now. When I return to the wheat-farming mecca where I was raised, I drive to the house my parents purchased long after I was on my own. It's an in-town address I looked up each year to mail them a package or card. But it still felt like home because the porch light was on, no matter what time we pulled into that quiet concrete drive.

LIGHTHOUSE PARENTING

My mother and dad have always been like author Kenneth Ginsburg's "lighthouse parents." Pillars in the close-knit community where I grew up. And they are who I've always known them to be.

According to Ginsburg, "lighthouse parenting" involves a stable presence on the shoreline a child can measure themselves against. Such parents look into the waves and trust children can eventually learn to ride those rough waters on their own.

A lighthouse stays in one place, a beacon that has ongoing communication with passing ships. From a known location, it warns of danger and provides informed guidance.

But it never chases down the ships.

I've had far-away people to meet and hard stops on my own path that were never part of my parents' desired itinerary for me. I can see now they must have bit their tongues and bound up their hearts each time as I moved farther and farther away from them. But Mom and Dad never stopped parenting me, whatever distance lay between us. They never required or pleaded that I move closer. They just gave wise advice. Sometimes I listened. Sometimes I didn't.

I'm now realizing how my parents lived the words of Gracy Olmstead, "This is the challenge of [parent]hood: to love wildly, fiercely, determinedly—and then, by God's grace, to let go."

THE LIGHT THAT GETS US HOME

This lighthouse analogy is more like how God parents His free-willed children.

And though lighthouses were all but unknown in Bible times, the Spirit used similar references to guiding lights. God led the Israelites through the desert nights using a pillar of fire. His illumination showed up at the consecration of Solomon's temple, and in a bush on Mt. Sinai. Once Jesus, the Light of the World, came on the scene, the Star of Bethlehem guided people to Him.

The only way any type of lighthouse works is if we know it's there, and reliable. Always working. Always on call. Then once our world goes dark, we instinctively look for its familiar illumination.

It is hardwired in every one of us to get back home to Him.

Even nights I wasn't home to see my parent's porch light, it was always on. Same with God's light. Times we're not turned toward Him, He's still there, beckoning us back.

PORCH LIGHTS WORK, TOO

Raised in landlocked Kansas, I didn't have much experience with lighthouses. But we all knew about porch lights.

A light on outside a neighbor's house meant…

You're welcome.

We're home.

We're awake if you need anything.

At your own house it meant…

We're waiting for you.

We're incomplete without you.

You always belong here.

The porch light was like a family's own lighthouse.

I was raised on this generous, stable light.

WE NEED THE DARK

Even so, somehow I expected a different kind of Parent when I was first diagnosed. I wanted God to direct me and the doctors, marionette-style. From my journal:

It's been four years since they declared my battered heart's function "near normal." Now, after several significant dips, I'm trying to understand what I should be learning from this. Truth is, people aren't supposed to survive the kind of heart failure I have. So this is all new ground for the doctors, like it is for me. I've been known to scream, "God please tell me or the doctors what to do next!" But no one has a map. I have a distinct feeling all of my life has been like that and I just didn't realize it. In my younger life, I thought God was directing me toward a story of blessing, and then once I got heart failure, toward a story of divine healing. Maybe my story has been more about preparing me for uncharted trust. Maybe every believer's story is.

When disease lingers and spouses leave, when jobs disappear and friends divorce, when children rebel and bad habits rule, it seems much easier for God to parachute in from a hovering aircraft. To fix it, or at least use the aircraft's loudspeaker to walk us through, to help us make all the correct turns so everything could be on course again.

Surely, He has a clearer perspective.

But Father God knows and my parents did, too, that preparation is the best protection. In fact, it's the only protection. We all need Someone who, from a foggy distance, we can still see. But darkness has to roll in or we never know the importance of the light source.

Rather than saving us from the storms, He prepares us to handle them.

Without turbulent teaching, I may never be able to navigate the choppy waters that surely still lie just out of view with my ongoing illness and my unmapped life.

And perhaps more importantly, there's a light we don't see until we're standing in the dark. We've left ours on plenty of times during the day, so I speak from experience. *We don't notice the porch light's beam on sunny days.*

Maybe that's why I'm just now understanding my parents' policy of parenting by porch light.

I'm learning that porch light parenting is what God modeled throughout the Bible and my parents modeled throughout my life: preparation and constancy in the beginning, and grace in the letting go.

RELIGHTING THE TRADITION

Turns out, that night I arrived late and the porch light was off, the bulb had actually burned out before I made it home. (Remember incandescents?) But I didn't figure that out until it was time to turn it on again for my dad or one of my brothers later that week. The bulb was replaced immediately and the porch light tradition continued.

Growing up, I didn't appreciate it, but regardless of any offense or difficulty between us, the porch light was a constant. As if continually extending grace to their children, Mom and Dad were to me the *parents of again.* As Beth Moore said of the ultimate Father, "Our God is the God of Again."

Like spring always waking up after a long winter.

God has shown up for us again and again, and He has forgiven us again and again for not showing up. Similarly, every night when one of our family members was out in the dangerous world, even long after we should have been, the porch light was lit again.

I may revive the porch light tradition in my own family. I have a new appreciation as a parent of far-flung children and as a wandering child of a constant God. A reformed helicopter parent, I feel like I've come full circle back to the porch light again. But I'm different this time. As Terry Pratchett says, "Coming back to where you started is not the same as never leaving."

Mom and Dad both passed away recently. I'll never again address a Mother's Day card or a Father's Day card. But even worse, now when we visit, the porch light is off, because we're arriving at an empty house, preparing it to sell.

I have a feeling I'll spend the rest of my life missing that extravagant gesture.

But while we're there for the weekend, in honor of all the children still on their journey, I'll be turning on that porch light myself.

DAY 37

Conquering the Stairs

I was petrified of those stairs.

When I was in kindergarten, my family moved into our unfinished basement while another story was added to our two-bedroom rancher. My mother took care of three children and a baby in that awkward, damp space for more than a year. We had a makeshift kitchen and beds for a family of six in the same room. Barely enough floor space to move around.

I remember the angst my parents expressed at the weather delays and construction snags.

I remember the rhyme my brother and sister made up about the absent builder.

I remember the historic snowfall that piled up past the clothesline that early spring.

But mostly, I remember the stairs.

Temporary stairs to the third floor were added early in the project. The gaping risers revealed the basement staircase directly beneath, and for a five-year-old, it was a long way down. My siblings loved to go to the "new upstairs" after the workers had left for the day. But my fear kept me a prisoner. I refused to go up, staying in the cocoon-like basement of safety for weeks.

Post-diagnosis, stairs have caused a pause in my confidence again. One of the most challenging parts of heart failure is shortness of breath, and inclines are my worst nemesis. But I'm finding that the root of the problem may actually be a spiritual one.

Often, the only way we get to what's next for us is uphill. After we cross a really scary flight of stairs. It was frightening, foreign territory to this kindergarten girl. And I'm not that different even today. I fear what's up ahead.

FEAR IS NATURAL BUT MUST BE SHORT-LIVED

Lately, I've found myself repeating the popular phrase, *Fear is a liar.* God did not give us a spirit of fear. But He did give us an emotion called fear. And then He hardwired it into us for survival.

Fear motivates us to act when peril is imminent—fight, flight, freeze. But in this age of information, we fear something even more than immediate danger. We fear something that can last our entire lives and keep us from fully developing our faith.

We fear what we don't know.

FEARING THE UNKNOWN

With TV streaming, my husband and I rarely see our college alma mater play in real time. We wait and watch it together, without network timeouts. I have to be honest; I usually check the internet to see who won so I know how the game is going to end beforehand. It doesn't spoil it for me, really. It helps me prepare. (That's what all control freaks say.)

So now in life I have this urge to speed through the commercials to the end, to see how an event plays out so I know how to live it. But I can't.

From my journal:

In the highest co-morbidity group with heart disease, I want to know this pandemic will end well for me and those I love. I want to know where my daughter will be next year for grad school. I want to know who my children will someday marry, where they'll live and work, how their lives will unfold. I want to know how effective my dad's chemo will turn out to be.

But none of that is mine to know or carry. Because sometimes what's at the top of those stairs may not be exactly what we've been praying for.

Most of what we fear never happens. But we all know some of it does. Job discovered this. "What I feared has come upon me; what I dreaded has happened to me" (Job 3:25 NIV).

God told us we should actually expect bad things to happen sometimes. Frederick Buechner put it this way: "Here is the world. Beautiful and terrible things will happen. Don't be afraid."

And so we struggle to live in it, especially when the incline is tough. This is not lost on our good God.

PERFECT LOVE DRIVES OUT FEAR

The Spirit urged several times after the bewildering resurrection, *Do not be afraid*. Sources say it appears as many as 365 times throughout the Bible.

I've never been sure how to just "not be afraid." But I'm starting to understand that, past our immediate, gut-level response, fear only has the power we give it. And we can choose to take our power elsewhere. Instead, we can invest our energy in love.

John was probably the last surviving apostle when he wrote these words, "perfect love drives out fear" (1 John 4:18b NIV). He had seen some of his worst fears realized, no doubt, in the horrible crucifixions and tortures of fellow apostles and dear friends. Yet, John talked about a perfect kind of love as the antidote.

And Jesus gave us the way to demonstrate that fear-eradicating love—a love for God and a love for others.

FOCUS ON GOD

Too often we see through to what could happen, to worst-case scenarios, instead of walking with our heads up and our hearts focused on Him. To love God, to tap into His fear-fighting glory, we have to keep Him in our line of vision.

Another apostle, Peter, had fear (and walking on water) conquered while his eye was on Jesus. He got into trouble when he lost sight of Jesus' hand. When he focused on the gaps in the stair risers or the rough water under him, fear sank Peter when he stopped trusting God to hold him.

Whatever we're facing, we can confidently give the frightening elevations to our all-knowing God. We will never find ourselves in a place He hasn't been. In a situation He doesn't know. In a circumstance He doesn't control.

Our God first walks on the rough water He asks us to navigate.

He always sits at the top of the stairs He wants us to climb.

So after we've had our moment of fight, flight, or freeze, we need to stop. Take a deep breath. And remind our souls who this God is.

And then we are uniquely prepared to be Jesus to others on the same stairs. It's the kingdom work we must do, even when (maybe mostly when) we are scared on the way to the new too.

CARE FOR OTHERS

One Friday afternoon, my sister devised a plan of covering the steps with towels so I couldn't see through them. As she coaxed me toward the new upstairs, she confided in me, "I was afraid the first time too." It worked, and on that day, for the first time in months, I saw my new bedroom.

While we're on that stairway, we need to help others. Especially the most vulnerable. We may have been born for such a time as this. Moments like these are what faith was designed for. To step out into this unique opportunity to serve and inspire. To love our at-risk neighbor as ourselves, even if we are healthy and life is humming along fine. To sympathize with others' unique fears. To find creative ways to assist those who struggle next to us on the stairs, just like my sister did for me.

After that first time, we never had to use the towels again. I bebopped up to the new upstairs dozens of times over the coming months.

Not because anything much changed for weeks during the historic snowstorm.

Not because the danger became a known quantity.

Because I stopped focusing on what *could* happen.

Because I had some vital help along the way.

DAY 38

When Doors Close

Admittedly, it was an ambitious bucket-list excursion.

Two years into my chronic, progressive disease we took a whirlwind trip overseas. I had never been outside the western hemisphere. So, despite my limited capability and life-altering fatigue, we decided I was finally doing well enough to take on the challenge.

One spot we landed was Rome, and specifically, the Vatican.

We marveled at the grandeur of the Sistine Chapel, the Raphael Room, and the Vatican museums. At one point inside St. Peter's Basilica, we decided to split up. My husband and daughter wanted to climb the 491 stairs to the top of the Dome, and knowing I couldn't, we set a meeting place and time to reconvene.

After admiring the artwork and architecture, I rounded a corner. Having entered early that morning, I was surprised at how the place had filled up. I joined a crowded line walking one direction, hoping to find the meeting place we had set. Before I realized what was happening, I was outside the building in the Piazza courtyard, along with what looked like hundreds of thousands of other people.

I immediately knew I needed to find a way inside to meet my family. But there was no getting back. My husband did not have international cell service on his phone. Only I did. How would they ever find me? *They'll think something horrible happened to me or that I had a medical emergency when I'm not at my designated place on time.*

I sent my husband a text message, sure that he would never receive it on the other side of that massive closed door.

DOORS CLOSE IN MANY WAYS

Some doors close softly, almost unnoticed. The job quietly goes to someone else, busyness slips us past the youth needed to chase our dreams.

Others slam shut:.

The building collapses.

The ventilator is switched off.

The moving van's ramp slides away.

The lot is sold.

Your ex remarries.

The unexpected hysterectomy happens.

The unbelievable amputation occurs.

We've all known doors that can never be reopened in this life, like casket lids and case files. We can pry or pound or plead, but the dead-bolt turns with a sickening thud.

Whether our plans fade away or are snatched in an instant, there is always a sound we can't get used to, inaudible but powerful, the din of a door closing. It often comes on the heels of hours, even years, of work and prayer and hope.

And following both the slam and the soft close, there is almost without exception, an even worse sound—God's silence.

WHEN GOD SAYS NO

After a dozen attempts to convince the guards to let me back in, they just quit talking to me. Tears, begging, explanations, nothing rocked the Vatican police. They silently gestured over to the entrance line, by then at least a four-hour wait. I panicked on one side of the huge doors while the only people I knew on the continent were on the other. With no way of reaching them, I did what any grown, reasonable person would do—I texted twenty-seven more times in a row. And after no response, I sat down alone in the blazing sun on St. Peter's Square and cried.

When doors close, not only does our caring God seem mute, we feel exiled, separated from the familiar. Just like the Israelites felt for forty years in the desert. We feel cut off from our comfort zone or divided from our dreams.

And it's particularly isolating when others have the door opened that you wanted open to you. *Why did God say no to me?*

When you're living a life you didn't want, it's not easy to accept the mystery of God's providence. We question His plan, His power. Even His presence.

The threshold of life's closed doors is where faith is tested.

NO EXPLANATION

With my unresolved heart failure, I've felt on the locked-out side of the door. I have repeatedly asked God to heal me and show His power, after all those who have stormed the gates of heaven on my behalf. He would get so much glory.

Like reasoning with the Vatican police…

It seemed an easy, quick fix.

I could see a clear way.

I could reason it out.

I had admirable, unselfish motives.

I wanted something good.

No one else would be harmed.

The Grantor would have looked merciful to allow it.

No amount of pleading or persuasion changed anything.

The soundless headshake said no. *You can't go back.*

On the lonely side of an immovable door, I've learned something about God's silence. As human beings, we're not ready to understand closed doors. As John Piper says, "Not until we walk through the open door and look back can we realize the necessity of all the other doors being closed." For some of us and some doors, that look-back won't happen this side of eternity.

In our lifetime God rarely, if ever, explains an impassable entry.

DOORS ALWAYS CLOSE FOR A REASON

The pages of the Bible are not lacking in closed doors that seemed so unexplained and so permanent when they first swung shut.

The gates of Paradise are locked.

The whale's jaws are clamped.

The fiery furnace door is latched.

Lazarus's tomb is sealed.

The lion's den entrance is fastened.

The stone to the Savior's tomb is placed.

On this side of history, these closed doors reveal purposes of protection, or redirection, or even affection. Biblical barred gates deepened man's connection to Him. It's easier to see now that certain doors had to remain closed to accomplish His plan.

And to get us ready for it.

Our good God is notorious for preparing His children for the task ahead while we wait behind closed doors…or while we reluctantly walk through different ones.

LIMITED IN LOVE

Sometimes God closes a door to mercifully intervene and limit our choice.

One of my greatest handicaps has always been having too many choices. From the 120-Crayola box to college majors to Netflix, I can become paralyzed by possibilities. Sometimes if doors don't close, we have too many unknowns, too many options, too many distractions.

A closed door can help us focus.

A fellow heart failure patient shared this piece of wisdom and it feels applicable to closed doors. "Not all storms come to destroy your life. Some storms come to clear your path." —Anonymous

I suspect that usually the closed door clears the way for something more important for us to do, or for a greater plan to begin unfolding. *Walk on down the hall. There's a better door ahead.* Without the benefit of a full explanation, we have to keep going to get to the perfect door. And bypass all the less-than-perfect closed ones.

Closed doors can actually be more gracious than open ones.

NEW OPPORTUNITIES

Thomas Carlisle, nineteenth-century essayist, wrote "When the oak tree is felled, the whole forest echoes with it. But one hundred acorns are planted silently by some unnoticed breeze."

I have felt the planting of those unwelcome acorns after doors were bolted and plans were toppled.

From my journal:

I can now appreciate how much of a life hinges on uncontrollable outcomes. I know I'm not alone: cancer, MS, Alzheimer's, all progress in leaps as the test result is opened.

"Holding steady," the doctor said. Good news. Still, I was sad. The little bit of my optimistic dad planted deep inside me hoped for a turn-around. Even though my cardiologist warned me years ago the door to improvement would remain closed.

As the doctor closed the door and left, my husband and I looked at each other and we both knew it. The good news is, she is no longer seeking life-saving measures for me. The bad news is, she is no longer seeking life-saving measures for me. I have moved from the emergent exam room to the chronic waiting room. With no more cutting-edge treatments on the horizon, I am left to cope as best I can, for as long as I can. In the middle of the thousands of patients and medical professionals at Cleveland Clinic that day, it felt like a lonely place to be.

NEVER REALLY ALONE

After that Vatican door wouldn't reopen, something else did. Up until that time, I had not been truly alone in my new diagnosis, without a way to contact my husband or loved ones. I was terrified I couldn't survive in that space. But I did. And after that, I was able to take bigger steps of independence, despite still having serious heart failure.

Nearly an hour after my series of frantic texts, my husband responded. They would be right out. They had a fantastic time. They never even knew I was locked out.

As is the case with God and closed doors, my husband got my messages and responded in due time. But it looked pretty dire on my side of the sealed entry. And that huge door never did open for me like I thought it should have.

Years ago, a much different door closed for me: the door to good health. It won't be reopening. At the same time, another entrance unlocked. With heart failure, there are many things I can no longer do, like standing and teaching college courses for hours at a time. But I found I can sit at a desk and type nearly the entire day. So, I finally started writing—something I never allowed myself the luxury to do in a healthier life.

And that's exactly what our Great Planner provides—another door. Even when we can't see it yet in our dark hallway. Even when we can see it and it's still not open, it will be, at precisely the perfect time. He has not abandoned us.

To be honest, most of the closed doors in my life are still a mystery. And I fully expect them to remain that way.

But I take comfort in this: He promises that one day closed doors will not exist (Revelation 3:8), as Jesus swings wide eternity's gate, "Enter into the joy of your master" (Matthew 25:21e ESV).

I don't know if it can qualify as a bucket-list item, but I'm sure looking forward to that.

DAY 39

A Desperate Reach

On my childhood farm, we birthed lots of litters of kittens. Often unintentionally. (To be fair, we needed barn and basement mousers,"and Bob Barker's warning was still several years out.) We had so many cats, we stopped naming them, and stopped missing them when they stopped showing up at the back door.

But puppies were a different story. Not sure if our dogs were routinely, covertly "fixed" or just not that fruitful, but a litter of new little dogs was a memorable event.

I have a clear recollection of secretly climbing huge round bales near the farmhouse, after overhearing Dad say our momma dog had her new family hidden near. I remember skipping across the careful rows, searching, then dropping down between scratchy rolls of hay to yelps of newborn pups, a ragtag bunch of excitement and energy. After a half hour of the face-licking fun, I began to regret my mischief. I wanted out of that claustrophobic environment. But I quickly learned I couldn't do it on my own. Getting down was one thing but getting back out was something else.

So I started yelling. Somehow, my dad heard me, and it wasn't long before the tip of his familiar boots appeared overhead. As he extended his worn, strong hand, I reached up and instantly knew I would be all right.

LORI ANN WOOD

OUR BEST HOPE

Reaching is something I've become familiar with throughout my lifetime. It is admitting we need more than our own arms can access—more resources, more reserves, more resilience.

That young puppy lover would later need to reach beyond her capability again, to desperately seek Him in the middle of a dire diagnosis.

From my journal:

I still reach out for my husband several times each night, just to know he's there. Heavy heart meds wield a cruel double-whammy. They bring unbelievable fatigue and also the inability to sleep soundly. After almost six years, I still wake up over and over, surprised to be the owner of this damaged heart. I didn't get the full, lasting recovery I wanted. I knew from the beginning it was a stretch, perhaps one that none of us could actually make, one none of us had a right to expect. Yet, somehow I still do.

Reaching says we can't do this on our own.

Reaching is the very act of believing.

The gospels tell of a desperate reacher too. Just three short verses in the book of Matthew.

"Just then a woman who had been subject to bleeding for twelve years came up behind him and touched the edge of his cloak. She said to herself, 'If I only touch his cloak, I will be healed.' Jesus turned and saw her. 'Take heart, daughter,' he said, 'your faith has healed you.' And the woman was healed at that moment" (Matthew 9: 20–22 NIV).

This woman with a chronic bleeding disorder that stumped the medical providers and drained her resources, grabbed the edge of Jesus' clothing in the middle of a crushing crowd. Her disease should have banned her from such a place. Yet she wove within the throng, pressing toward Jesus. Each person who bumped into her could have become unclean, too—including Him. She took a massive risk entering that scene. But, after twelve years of suffering, she was desperate for a miracle. Coming close enough to see Jesus, she stretched her entire wounded self toward Him.

Like a drowning person reaching through waves, or a swallowed up little girl reaching through the hay. Reaching for a lifeline by touching the edge of her Father's attire.

This short saga is one of the buried treasures of the gospel. But there are other similar stories of boundary crossers, who like reachers, will do anything to get to Jesus. They push through any barrier to be near Him.

Jewish leader Jairus risking humiliation in hopes of healing for his daughter.

Faithful friends digging through a neighbor's roof then lowering a paralyzed man to the Healer.

Blind Bartimaeus shouting at the top of his lungs for Jesus' touch as the crowd tries to hush him.

The unwelcome woman with her jar of precious perfume, barging into a house just to pour her life savings on the Savior's head.

Each desperate person's part was small but risky, a reach, an ask, an entry, a pour.

Hoping I wouldn't be scolded for the unapproved puppy visit, I risked it too. And Dad might never have found me between the bales without my courageous yell.

Any time we're in an unscalable chasm, a dangerous reach toward our Father is our best hope.

REACHING FOR A BETTER END

We've all been this bleeding believer, a desperate outcast who dared reach out to a busy Man, with a deep conviction He could help. And a spark of hope He would.

Faith grows when we step forward in the dark, or reach out in fear or even in doubt. When we have no other option.

Sometimes this desperate faith is the strongest, truest kind.

Cleaning out Dad's closet after his passing, I found an "As Seen on TV" grabber tool I didn't know he owned, and I smiled. It seemed so appropriate. I watched him reach for God the last few years of his life. Because I was reaching with him. It's instinctively what we do when we're in trouble.

If only I could touch Him.

"It's uncomfortable, even excruciating, to long for something just out of reach, to graze a toe but never catch hold of that which you hope and believe will make everything right." —Teri Ott

But real hope was never meant to be easy or comfortable.

And the Spirit wanted us to know that being in a position to reach is how we get hope in the first place. "[W]e also glory in our sufferings, because we know that suffering produces perseverance; perseverance, character; and character, hope" (Romans 5:3–4 NIV).

I've snagged some of this hard-won hope as my suffering arms stretch toward Him and a better tomorrow.

"Hope isn't what I thought it was: a story about us. Instead, it's a story about God that's dropped like an anchor in the future. God is pulling us toward it, and that feels like a someday in which there will be no more tears." —Kate Bowler

The very essence of hope is reaching past what is, toward what could be.

Hope does the hard work of wanting grandchildren, a legacy, a long life, when it looks uncertain. When we reach, we're hoping to grab a different conclusion to our circumstance.

For all of us who, in hope of healing or a second chance, have ever touched the hem of the medical system, or the court system, or the school system:

We are looking for a better end to our story.

WHAT WE GRASP

Often the word used for *healing* in the New Testament means something closer to "made whole" or even "forgiven." It seems spiritual wholeness, rather than physical relief, should be our highest hope in reaching out to God. And it seems it's always more about His constant companionship than our current condition.

"In the middle of things seemingly not working out *for* us, God is working out something *in* us." —Ann Voskamp

The hard truth is, we may reach and not get ahold of what we first wanted or asked for. We don't always get a better end to the earthbound chapter of our story. But we always get a clearer view of our God. Like the bleeding woman in the Bible, a reach first touches His hem, but it ultimately turns our heart to Him.

On my best days, I'm a reacher too.

And bit by bit, with each attempted grasp, I'm starting to see this God who my prayers constantly reach for. So maybe the desperate reach has always been less about pulling me *out* and more about pulling Him *in*.

When Dad showed up at the top of those hay bales, I was relieved to see him. As he reached in to pull me out, his broken-in farm boots slipped and he ended up down with the wiggly ones too.

As Dad picked up a tiny pup and put it in his pocket, I knew I was experiencing a better ending to my story.

Suddenly, like with my heart failure, it didn't matter so much about getting out.

I was content since my Father was right there with me.

DAY 40

A Charge to Keep Questioning

Today, this final day of the journey, it now begins to dovetail with yours. I set out to write this story not because it is terribly rare, but because it is terribly common. I wrote it for every wounded believer, afraid or even ashamed, to question on this path they didn't choose.

It was never my goal for you to be content just reading my story. My purpose is to impact and empower you to live a better version of your own.

So, where this book ends, your revised story begins. I can assure you that your plotline, like mine, will include more detours. But in those desert places, something amazing can happen: A new chapter is written where questions build your faith rather than destroy it, where God is not afraid of your questions, and where you fully expect to confront the uncertainties of worry, doubt, and control.

Even embracing the questions, deserts can be harsh, unforgiving places. We all know that sometimes the desert detour lasts longer than we'd like. Several years ago, I thought I was about to get my life back. I thought my old normal had returned for good. I thought I was healed from heart failure. From my journal:

We got amazing news at Cleveland Clinic. The heart that doctors said could never heal, somehow got better. The depression I was warned about never arrived. The meds that were supposed to bottom out my blood pressure never did. The trial that should have stolen my faith only strengthened it.

I just knew that was the end to my detour and my questioning. But two years later, when I was in chronic heart failure again, I felt the familiar feeling of being caught in something too big to understand.

Questions of worry, doubt, and control returned. But they were not strangers to me by then. I welcomed them in. We wrestled again and I grew stronger in my faith. The same will happen for you. Although this hasn't been your story, in many ways it has. It is the story of every believer who trudges through this broken world toward a better one.

The beautiful part is we are never on the detour alone. Jesus bought that for us and He lived it for us. Describing Jesus' time in the desert, Matthew 4:11 and Mark 1:13 both assure us that angels attended Him. The Spirit also goes with us, to guide us into all truth (John 16:13).

But Luke 4:13 warns that the Enemy will be back, too, at our lowest and most vulnerable times. Detours to the desert will still come; difficult questions will resurface. And while Satan wants to use those questions to separate us from God, the Spirit intends to use them to bring us closer to Him. Just as Jesus' painful time in the desert launched his history-defining ministry, the days in the desert can refresh your faith and revamp your story.

To embrace a new, unplanned chapter, we have to know and trust the Author.

Jesus was able to handle His human struggles in the desert because He knew God's stories and He knew God's words. He responded to each of the Enemy's whispers, "It is written." Jesus leaned on the promises He knew from the God who led His well-loved children through a different desert with Moses.

Now Jesus invites us all into that same intimate knowing in our own desert. Yet Jesus understands, no matter how deep the knowing, uncertainties will remain. Such is the nature of authentic faith.

We are a people with questions. According to the Pew Research Center and the Barna Group, in the US adult professing-Christian population, nearly two-thirds question God or their faith at some point in their journey. And deep within these questions is where faith is fortified. Francis Bacon in *The Advancement of Learning* said, "If we begin with certainties, we will end in doubt, but if we begin with doubts and bear them patiently, we may end in certainty."

The questions you've explored in this book are the three that every life must confront. Three questions that every life *will* confront, one way or another. It happens when humanity encounters divinity, like the human-nature of Jesus pleading with God the Father in the desert. In our limited capacity to comprehend, we ask. And our all-knowing God is not afraid of the questions. He encourages them. He begs us to ask so He can answer. As Timothy Adkins-Jones said, "we serve a God who refuses to allow the conversation to end."

Our job is to never stop asking the hard questions, to engage in the faith struggles, and to trust the detours to the God who can handle it all.

The God who gives us an eternal perspective to overcome our worries.

The God who has already proven He is the God of boundless love and trustworthiness.

The God whose long-term perspective and plan far overshadow our own.

Expect the detours. And most importantly, keep asking the questions. They will keep your faith alive.

Acknowledgments

This book began as a reluctant hospital journal, prompted by my husband in my most difficult, early hours. It grew to include stories of my past, ones I came to realize were, in ways only God could design, part of everyone's past. The sum of these stories, and the questions they addressed, became much grander and far-reaching than I could have imagined that first dark day in ICU.

As the project is completed, I have more emotions than space.

I am humbled by those who have unselfishly and extravagantly poured their early support into me. Though I can't name each one here, you are known.

I am thankful for mentors who took a naïve accountant and molded her into a writer: Kathy Izard, Chad Allen, Jonathan Merritt, Margaret Feinberg, The Word Girls, *The Joyful Life* staff, and though he never knew it, Frederick Buechner.

I am honored to claim as my own several families that never stopped believing even when I couldn't: my family of readers, my family of friends, my church family, the family I grew up with, and the family I am growing old with.

I am blessed to have in my circle a host of medical angels:

- Dr. Gary Neaville, who cared for my entire family for decades, and who, even in retirement, follows my health journey;
- Dr. Christopher Simpson, who was the first to believe I could survive, and took brave steps to keep me alive;
- Nurse Practitioner Heather Rothrock-Heltemes, who from the

moment we met, cared for me as a best friend would, and delivered both the worst and the best news of my life with genuine compassion;

- Dr. Eileen Hsich, whose skill and care in cardiology first gave me hope, then saved my life, and ultimately made this book possible;
- Dr. Khaldoun Tarakji, who took on a risky case and then refused to give up on me in the middle of a difficult surgery;
- Sonographer Evelina Petrovets who dared connect world-class medical care with world-changing prayer;
- Nurses in clinics, hospitals, ICUs, ERs, and cardiac rehabs, who, nameless but not faceless, carried me through my worst moments.

I am indebted to Mercy Hospital Northwest Arkansas Cardiology, Cleveland Clinic Cardiology, WomenHeart and the American Heart Association who fight every day not just for me but for the world population, to unseat heart disease as our number one killer, and turn heart failure into a detour instead of a death sentence.

I am grateful for the women of CrossRiver Media, Tamara Clymer, Debra Butterfield, and DeeDee Lake, who saw potential in my work to make a difference for others on a path they didn't choose.

About the Author

Lori Ann Wood lives in the shadow of the Ozark Mountains in beautiful Bentonville, Arkansas, with her husband, the unsuspecting guy she chased all the way from ninth grade to grad school. She is mom to three world-changing young adults, one impressive son-in-law (who all live too far away) and a miniature dachshund named Pearl (who threatens to never leave). Her newest obsession is her granddaughter Hazel.

Lori Ann is a WomenHeart Champion Community Educator and an American Heart Association Ambassador. She also serves on the Blog Contributor Team for *The Joyful Life Magazine*. In addition to receiving the Frederick Buechner Narrative Essay Award, and awards from the Colorado Christian Writers and the Evangelical Press Association, her work has been published in numerous print journals, including *The Christian Century Magazine, Just Between Us Magazine, The Joyful Life Magazine, Bella Grace Magazine, Heart Insight Magazine, Sweet to the Soul FAITH Magazine,* and *Truly Magazine*. Her articles have also appeared on websites such as *The New York Times, Pepperdine University Press, Yahoo Lifestyle, MSN,* and *NewsFlash*, and on blogs including *Women | Faith & Story, Kindred Mom, WomenHeart,* and *The Mighty*.

But Lori Ann has not always been a writer.

A life detour reordered her priorities and rattled her faith.

In 2015, despite otherwise pristine health, Lori Ann almost died from heart failure from an unknown cause.

Having discovered this chronic, progressive condition almost too late, Lori Ann now writes to encourage difficult faith questions along the detours of life. Her passion is to connect with readers and help them hold onto their faith when they find themselves on a path they didn't choose.

Get her free guide for staying close to God in hard times at https://loriannwood.com/hope.

BIG STEPS
LITTLE STEPS
Moving forward in our walk with God
Available in bookstores and from online retailers.
CrossRiver Media
www.crossrivermedia.com

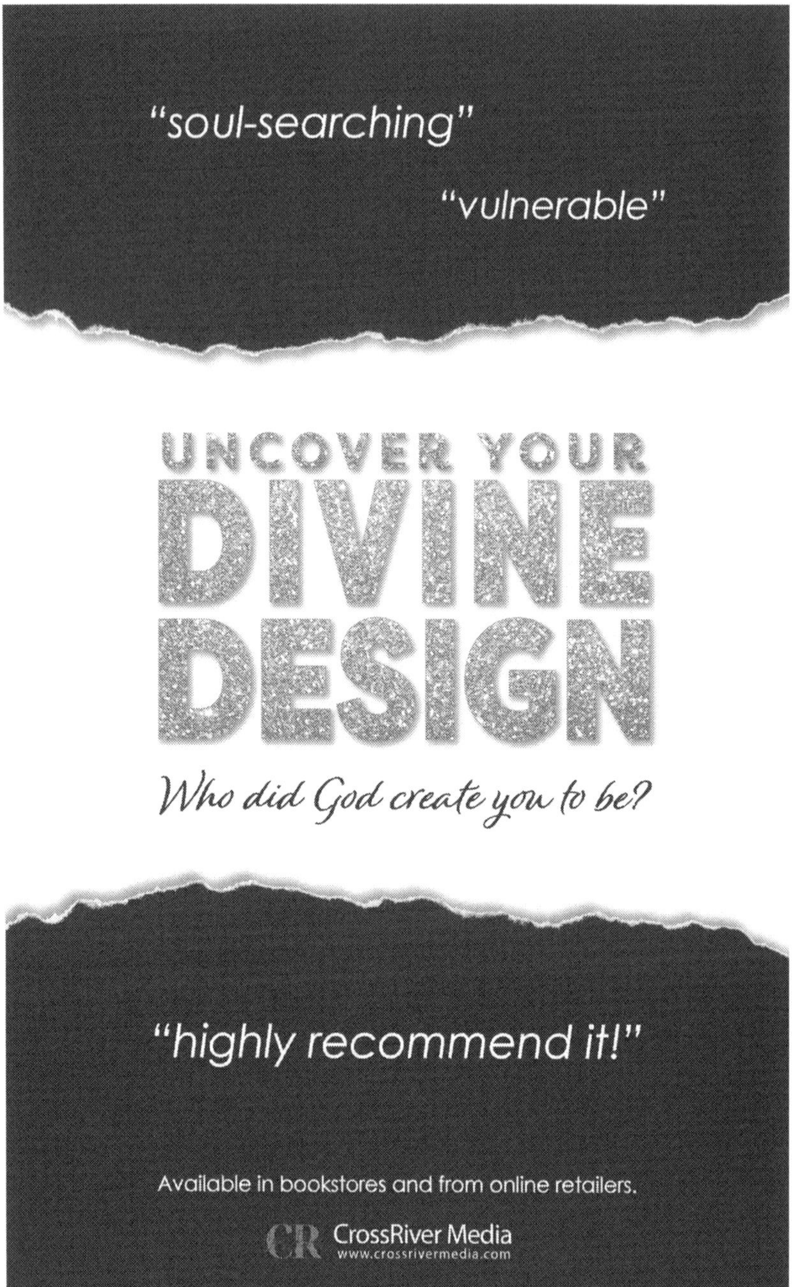
"soul-searching"
"vulnerable"
UNCOVER YOUR
DIVINE DESIGN
Who did God create you to be?
"highly recommend it!"
Available in bookstores and from online retailers.
CrossRiver Media
www.crossrivermedia.com

If you enjoyed this book, will you consider sharing it with others?

- Please mention the book on Facebook, Instagram, Pinterest, or another social media site.
- Recommend this book to your small group, book club, and workplace.
- Head over to Facebook.com/CrossRiverMedia, 'Like' the page and post a comment as to what you enjoyed the most.
- Pick up a copy for someone you know who would be challenged or encouraged by this message.
- Write a review on your favorite ebook platform.
- To learn about our latest releases subscribe to our newsletter at CrossRiverMedia.com.

Made in the USA
Columbia, SC
17 February 2023

12566348R00128